The Fast-Track MBA Series

Co-published with AMED (the Association f
Development

CW01501214

Consultant Edit
John Kind, Director, Harbridge
David Megginson, Associate Head, S.

THE FAST-TRACK MBA SERIES represents an innovative and refreshingly different approach to presenting core subjects in a typical MBA syllabus in a lively and accessible way. The usual text book approach is eschewed in favour of a practical, action-oriented style which involves the reader in self-assessment and participation.

Ideal for managers wanting to renew or develop their management capabilities, the books in *THE FAST-TRACK MBA SERIES* rapidly give readers a sound knowledge of all aspects of business and management that will boost both self-confidence and career prospects. For those fortunate enough to take an MBA, the *Series* will provide a solid grounding in the subjects to be studied. Managers and students worldwide will find this new series an exciting and challenging alternative to the usual study texts and management guides.

Titles already available in the series are:

★ *Strategic Management* (Robert Grant & James Craig)
★ *Organisational Behaviour and Design* (Barry Cushway & Derek Lodge)
★ *Problem Solving and Decision Making* (Graham Wilson)
★ *Human Resource Development* (David Megginson, Jennifer Joy-Matthews & Paul Banfield)
★ *Accounting for Managers* (Graham Mott)

Forthcoming books in the series will cover:

Data Analysis and IT ★ Financial Management ★ Human Resource Management ★ International Management ★ Investment and Risk ★ Law ★ Business Ethics ★ Economics ★ Marketing ★ Operations Management.

AMED is an association of individuals who have a professional interest in the development of people at work. AMED's network brings together people from industry, the public sector, academic organizations and consultancy, and is exclusive to individuals.

The aims of AMED are to promote best practice in the fields of individual and organizational development, to provide a forum for the exploration of new ideas, to offer members opportunities for their own development and to encourage the adoption of ethical practices in development.

For further information on AMED you are invited to write to AMED, 21 Catherine Street, London WC2B 5JS.

The Series Editors

John Kind is a director of Harbridge House, a consultancy firm specializing in management development and training. He has wide experience of designing and presenting business education programmes in various parts of the world for clients such as BAA, Bass, British Petroleum and General Electric. John Kind is a visiting lecturer at Henley Management College and holds an MBA from the Manchester Business School and an honours degree in Economics.

David Megginson is a writer and researcher on self-development and the line manager as developer. He has written *A manager's Guide to Coaching, Self-development: A Facilitator's Guide, Human Resource Development* in the Fast-track MBA series, *The Line Manager as Developer* and the *Developing the Developers* research report. He consults and researches in blue chip companies, and public and voluntary organizations. He is a director of the European Mentoring Centre and an elected Council member of AMED, and has been Associate Head of Sheffield Business School and a National Assessor for the National Training Awards.

Sally Yeung, Partner, Lansdell Associates, is a freelance writer, editor and translator. Previously director of the Association for Management Education and Development and Research Associate at Ashridge Strategic Management Centre, she is the author of books and articles on mission and corporate philosophy, organization development, managing change and Japanese management.

Accounting for Managers

G R A H A M   M O T T

Published in association with AMED

KOGAN
PAGE

First published in 1994

Kogan Page Limited
120 Pentonville Road
London N1 9JN

© Graham Mott, 1994

British Library Cataloguing in Publication Data

A CIP record for this book is available from the British Library.

ISBN 0 7494 1216 X

Typeset by Saxon Graphics Ltd, Derby
Printed and bound in Great Britain by Biddles Ltd, Guildford and Kings Lynn

Contents

Foreword by Sir John Egan

Every business succeeds by satisfying the needs of its customers. Managers have therefore to refresh continually their understanding of their customers' requirements and anticipate shifts in demand and expectations.

One thing does, however, tend to remain constant. Customers want good quality and low cost. So the managerial challenge is to deliver products and services efficiently, profitably and to high standards of quality so that the enterprise can prosper.

Of course all competitive businesses must also seek to continually raise their standards of customer satisfaction. The marketplace continues to widen, and in many sectors is already global, and the cost of entry to markets tends to decrease. Businesses must respond by continuously improving themselves.

These simple, even obvious, principles can be very difficult to put into practice, but in Britain we have now started to learn from the experience of others, such as Germany and Japan, by improving our managerial processes.

The most vital contributor to Continuous Improvement is the manager. All managers have to ensure that their own education and training is sufficient for the business challenges of both today and tomorrow. Relying solely on learning by experience on the job will leave too much to chance. The successful manager of the future will accept responsibility for his or her own development, and the development of their staff.

The Fast Track MBA series should be an invaluable aid to the manager who wants to improve personal performance and to plan for long-term success.

Sir John Egan
Chief Executive, BAA plc

Acknowledgements

I wish to thank the following organizations for permission to reproduce accounting statements from their annual report and accounts:

British Gas plc
City of Newcastle upon Tyne
John Menzies plc
Northern Electric plc

Most of this book is applicable to any form of business organization, but the profit-seeking private sector is taken as the main source of examples with illustrations of other sectors added for comparison where appropriate. I hope you enjoy it and find it useful in getting to grips with financial matters.

I would also like to draw readers' attention to the many topical and useful articles contained in two magazines in particular. *Accountancy* is the monthly journal of The Institute of Chartered Accountants in England and Wales. It covers all aspects of accounting and finance but is particularly useful for keeping abreast of developments in financial reporting.

Management Accounting is the monthly journal of The Chartered Institute of Management Accountants of which I am an associate member. As the title suggests, it is very helpful in giving information about new ideas in management accounting.

Readers are directed to particular articles in these magazines and elsewhere at the end of most chapters, as well as to research studies sponsored by the accounting profession.

Finally I would like to thank Valerie, my wife, for her forbearance and for her help in editing the text yet again.

Graham Mott
April 1994

Part One
Financial accounting

Accounting has a language of its own with a variety of statements and jargon guaranteed to mystify the manager who has not taken time out to learn about them. A basic knowledge of the three key statements of profit and loss account or other income statement, balance sheet and cash flow are essential if we are to communicate sensibly with colleagues, subordinates and financial people. We also need to understand fully the part we play in achieving satisfactory financial results for our organization.

In recent years it has been suggested that many well-known companies have been putting the best face on their financial performance by the use of what is now called 'creative accounting'. Indeed, whole books have been written on this topic alone. If you want to know what all the fuss has been about, try reading Smith's *Accounting for growth*, listed in the Bibliography.

There has also been a debate among accountants, heads of companies and others about the meaning and purpose of the balance sheet statement in particular. This raises questions of how to value tangible assets when the purchasing power of money changes over time and how to value intangible assets like goodwill and brand values.

Some companies have jumped the gun by incorporating brand values in their balance sheet list of assets. Members of the accounting profession are critical of the continuing use of historic cost accounting which may mislead some users of the statement, but past memories of the problems following the trial of current cost accounting in the early 1980s suggest we should proceed with caution.

All this, plus a few major scandals such as BCCI, Polly Peck and Maxwell, have called into question the reliability and purpose of companies' annual accounts. We now have the Cadbury Report recommending a 'code of best practice' concerning the financial aspects of corporate governance. The Accounting Standards Board is tightening up financial reporting with the issue to date of four Financial Reporting Standards, one of which deals with the reporting of financial performance (ie the profit and loss account) and another with the presentation of the cash flow statement. If you are new to the subject, the Glossary at the back of the book will help you to understand the most important accounting definitions and terms.

1

Financial reporting

Your organization will disclose financial information to outside parties in its annual report and accounts. This report contains the three key financial statements of:

- income statement (a profit and loss account, or revenue account, or income and expenditure account);
- balance sheet;
- cash flow statement.

If you work for a quoted public company, this is updated by an interim report informing shareholders of the company's half-year figures, the proposed dividend, a review of current trading and the financial position.

The Corporate Report[1] identified the following user groups as having a reasonable right to financial information from medium and large companies, central government, local authorities, charities and other bodies:

- *Shareholders*—both existing and potential investors need information to help them decide whether to hold, buy or sell shares in a company.
- *Loan creditors*—they need to assess any risk to the interest payments on the loans and the eventual capital repayment of the loans.
- *Employees*—individuals and their representatives need information to assess job security, job prospects and to aid collective bargaining.
- *Analysts and advisers*—the financial press, the City and financial advisers generally need access to financial information to advise their readers and clients.

- *Business contacts*—trade creditors, customers and competitors are all interested in an organization's financial performance, standing and future prospects.
- *Government*—in addition to government perhaps being a customer or creditor, the taxation of profits requires very specific disclosure of certain financial information.
- *Public*—information supplied to shareholders and business contacts should satisfy needs regarding employment and wealth creation issues.

THE REGULATORY FRAMEWORK

There are no limits to the amount of financial information that can be disclosed to shareholders, employees, suppliers etc, but there are minimum disclosure requirements laid down and accounting policies to be observed. These requirements are contained in:

- Companies Acts;
- financial reporting standards (FRSs);
- statements of standard accounting practice (SSAPs);
- Cadbury Committee report on *Financial aspects of corporate governance*;[2]
- Stock Exchange listing requirements;
- international accounting standards (IAS);
- generally accepted accounting practice (GAAP).

Companies Acts

The 1985 Act consolidated much previous legislation and was amended by the 1989 Act which contains most of the requirements to align the UK with EC practice as far as possible.

Accounting standards

Financial reporting standards are a relatively new response by the accountancy profession to the need to tighten up the rules and impair the use of creative accounting. These will augment, or in some cases completely replace, the older statements of standard accounting practice.

To date, only four new FRSs have been issued dealing with the cash flow statement, accounting for subsidiary undertakings, reporting financial performance (ie the profit and loss account), and accounting for capital instruments. Kirk, in his article 'Accounting standards: the pace of change accelerates',[3] provides a useful update on standard setting, although it must be recognized that this is a fast-moving field.

A multinational company will need to design accounting systems which comply with both the accounting regulations in the various countries in which it operates and the requirements of the stock exchanges on which it is listed. There is not yet accounting harmony in the EU, let alone in the world, notwithstanding the existence of international accounting standards.

If this area interests you, try reading the article by Lawrence on 'The diversity of accounting in a single Europe'.[4] On the global front, Cairns' article 'The IASC – 20 more years of vision and commitment'[5] provides a useful update on worldwide standard setting.

Regulation

Auditors can be viewed as the front-line troops which ensure organizations comply with legislation and reporting standards.

As a last resort, the Financial Reporting Review Panel can take legal action against companies which refuse to comply with the standards and/or legal requirements. The Stock Exchange can suspend the quotation of any listed company that does not comply with its rules on disclosure. The Registrar of Companies can fine directors of companies who do not file proper accounts within the stipulated time periods. According to the DTI's annual report, the compliance rate in June 1993 was 88 per cent—an improvement on the previous year, no doubt due to the imposition of penalties for late filing!

Such sanctions add bite to the relatively new FRSs aimed at tightening up reporting standards and making accounting statements more informative, even if this is at the expense of their being more complicated to read. The code on corporate governance has the backing of the stock exchange but is not, as yet, enforceable. Finance directors of large companies have successfully pleaded that they are having to cope with so much change at once with all the new standards coming into force that they are unable to cope with all the Cadbury requirements.

Generally accepted accounting practice (GAAP)

GAAP refers to all the rules and regulations governing accounting. In the UK this embraces UK and foreign (particularly US) company law,

UK and international accounting standards and Stock Exchange requirements. GAAP is merely a descriptive term and has no legal authority itself. As legislation and standards are constantly changing in the UK and abroad, so GAAP itself is always changing.

ACCOUNTING CONVENTIONS

The three main financial statements, namely the income statement, balance sheet and cash flow statement, are prepared to inform management and owners about the financial performance and position of an organization. Accountants produce these statements to comply with the legal and professional requirements discussed above, and also follow various accounting conventions or principles, of which the main ones are:

■ separate entity;
■ money measurement;
■ going concern;
■ consistency;
■ prudence;
■ profit;
■ accrual accounting;
■ revenue expenditure;
■ capital expenditure;
■ depreciation;
■ historical cost accounting.

If you are to understand financial statements, some justification for the existence of these conventions is required.

Separate entity

Every business is regarded as a separate entity in order that its financial performance can be measured. This requires accountants to keep its financial transactions separate from those of both its owners and other businesses.

Money measurement

Only transactions with a monetary value can be recorded. Money is the common denominator that allows us to aggregate transactions, as when we add the sales of different products and services together to get one total sales value. Internally generated goodwill and brand values built up over long periods of time have a monetary value, but are difficult to measure. At the time of writing, these items are the subject of intense debate as to whether they should appear as assets in the company balance sheet and, if so, on what basis they should be valued.

Going concern

Assets are normally valued on the assumption that the business will continue to exist and carry on trading. In a forced sale or liquidation, an asset such as work in progress may fetch a very different value to that shown in the company's balance sheet.

Consistency

The basis on which information is prepared and presented should be consistent from year to year to enable true comparisons to be made. One example of this relates to depreciation (see below). Organizations should apply the same depreciation method and rates from one year to the next so that performance is not affected by changes in policy.

Prudence

The convention of prudence dictates that income and profit should not be anticipated, but should be included in the profit and loss account when realized, either in the form of cash or some other asset of equivalent value, for example a customer debt. Conversely, provision should be made for all known liabilities and future losses, even if the exact amount is not known with certainty. Taken together, this is often loosely interpreted as 'accountants never anticipate profits before they are earned, but they do anticipate losses before they have occurred!'

Profit

The difference in value between sales revenue and the expenses consumed on gaining those sales in a period of time is called profit, which represents an increase in the owners' wealth. The American term for profit is 'income'. Conversely, a loss is a reduction in owners' wealth caused by expenses exceeding sales revenue in the period.

Accrual accounting

Accrual accounting establishes the principle that expenses and revenue are included in the period in which they are due, not when they are actually paid or received. For this reason, *the profit earned in a period is not the same as the cash generated* in that same period.

The timing of exactly when a sale takes place is crucial to the measurement of performance over short time periods like a month. In most cases the sale of goods or services is deemed to take place on delivery and invoice, not when cash is received.

Exceptions to this rule include long-term contract work by civil engineers and contractors who receive monthly progress payments as work progresses. Sales turnover in their case is the value of work done in each month, which avoids the need to wait for the value of the whole job to be determined on completion. Thus the distortion of periodic results is kept to the minimum.

Estimates of uninvoiced goods and services are referred to as *'accruals'*. You may provide such information to your organization's accountants at the end of each month for inclusion in that month's profit and loss account. Somewhat similar to an accrual is a *'provision'*. This relates to a liability or a loss which is likely to occur, but for which the amount and/or the future date are uncertain. A provision for deferred tax, a provision for restructuring costs and a provision for bad debts are common examples which are explained later.

Revenue expenditure

All expenditure is classified as either revenue expenditure or capital expenditure. Revenue expenditure refers to expenditure consumed in a period of time and charged against revenue in the profit and loss account or other income statement for that period. It usually includes:

■ labour costs;
■ material costs;
■ overhead expenses for services and other running costs.

Capital expenditure

Capital expenditure is expenditure on long-life assets which the organization uses itself in its business and which are not intended for sale to its customers. It includes:

■ land and buildings;
■ plant, machinery and equipment;

- motor vehicles;
- fixtures and fittings.

Depreciation

Depreciation relates to the spreading of the cost of a long-life asset over its expected life, and has two effects. First, the value of the asset is gradually reduced by the cumulative depreciation in the balance sheet and secondly, the depreciation for a single period is included as an expense in the income statement.

Example

A machine is bought for £20,000 and is expected to last five years. Depreciation of £4000 will be included with other expenses in the income statement for the first year and the machine's value shown as £16,000 in the balance sheet at the year-end. By the end of the second year the balance sheet value will have fallen to £12,000 after a further £4000 depreciation has been charged in the income statement for that year.

Historical cost accounting (HCA)

You may be surprised to learn that assets are disclosed in a balance sheet at their original cost less depreciation based on that same historical cost. This is an example of accountants using actual figures in preference to subjective estimates, even if those actuals are now out of date! The use of HCA does not preclude the revaluation of valuable land and buildings from time to time, without going so far as to revalue all assets as required in current cost accounting. We explore this issue further in a later chapter.

HCA usually has the effect of understating asset values in the balance sheet owing to the impact of inflation over long periods of time. HCA also overstates profit in the income statement because of the inadequate depreciation charge, as this is calculated on the original cost of the asset as opposed to its current replacement cost.

DOUBLE ENTRY BOOKKEEPING

It might seem strange to include a section on bookkeeping in a textbook for managers. If you are familiar with the topic then please skip this section. Its inclusion is quite deliberate, since the underlying principles of bookkeeping provide a number of very useful explanations, for example:

- Why does a balance sheet always balance?
- Where do accountants get all the details from to produce the accounts?
- How do accountants know how much each customer owes?

Unless you work in the smallest of organizations, a system of recording called *double entry bookkeeping* will be employed. This system records both cash and credit transactions when they arise at their different times. The term double entry derives from the fact that each individual transaction is entered twice, recognizing two aspects of the same transaction. These two aspects are referred to by accountants as *debits* and *credits*.

Years ago, when all firms recorded transactions in books or ledgers, the left side was the debit side and the right the credit side. On the left side were all the expense items and assets of value to the business; on the right side the sources of income and any liabilities to repay money in the future. Cash received went on the left and cash paid out on the right. To summarize:

Debit side	*Credit side*
Expenses consumed	Sales or revenue or turnover
Assets (including customer debts)	Liabilities (including debts to suppliers)
Cash received	Cash paid out

Confusion is sometimes created when we think of our bank manager telling us that our account is in credit, meaning that we have money deposited in the account. From our point of view such money is an asset—a debit balance. From the bank's point of view, money owed to us is a liability—a credit balance. Debit and credit are reversed between the two parties involved. Likewise, a trade creditor in a customer's books is a trade debtor in its supplier's books and vice versa.

Accounts are opened in a ledger for each type of expense, asset, sales and liability. These are listed in a *chart of accounts* and identified by code numbers, as explained in Chapter 7.

Visualize an account as a letter T, with the name of the account on the crossbar and any entries of figures on the left or the right side of the vertical bar. Each financial transaction is entered twice in a double entry system, once in two separate accounts. One entry will be on the debit (left) side in one account, while the other entry will always be on the credit (right) side of the second account involved. Let us take a few simple examples.

Example 1 Paid £200 wages on Aug 2 with money drawn from the bank account.

Wages a/c

Aug 2   Bank a/c   200 |

Bank a/c

                        | Aug 2   Wages a/c   200

Wages are an expense so the entry goes on the debit side of that account. Notice that the other account involved is always given as the cross-reference in addition to the date of the transaction. Cash paid out for any reason is always a credit entry in the bank account, as shown above.

Double entry bookkeeping copes equally well with credit transactions and allows organizations to keep track of monies owing to any supplier or customer.

Example 2 Purchased £900 goods on credit from A Supplier on Aug 5.

Purchases a/c

Aug 5   A Supplier a/c   900 |

A Supplier a/c

                        | Aug 5   Purchases a/c 900

The two accounts involved here are the purchases account (an expense item) and that of A Supplier (a liability). Notice that every credit customer and every supplier will have their own separate account so we can keep track of all amounts owing to and by the business for each party individually.

Example 3 On Aug 29, A Supplier is paid £600 on account.

A Supplier a/c

Aug 29   Bank a/c   600 |

Bank a/c

                        | Aug 29   A Supplier a/c 600

Cash paid out again goes on the credit side of the bank account while the other entry shows the liability to the supplier being reduced by the amount paid. This will become clearer shortly when we look at the supplier's account in full.

THE TRIAL BALANCE

At the end of an accounting period, usually the month end, each account is balanced off and all balances then listed in a *trial balance*. In the case of the wages account, there may be four or five entries on the debit side during any one month. The balance on this account is the total of all those entries on the same side.

In the case of the above supplier's account, there are entries on both sides of the same account. In this case the balance is the amount by which the greater side exceeds the smaller side. This is now shown as £300.

A Supplier a/c

Aug 29	Bank a/c	600	Aug 5	Purchases a/c	900
			Aug 31	Balance	300

All accounts are balanced off at the end of the month in this way, and those with a balance are then listed in the trial balance. In the few accounts we entered transactions in above, the trial balance would come out like this:

Trial balance as at 31 August 199x

Debit balances:	£	*Credit balances:*	£
Purchases a/c	900	Bank a/c	800
Wages a/c	200	A Supplier	300
	£1100		£1100

Trial balances must always balance because identical amounts have been entered on opposite sides in two different accounts, and when an account is balanced off, an equal amount is cancelled out on each side to strike the balance. The trial balance, therefore, goes some way to proving the accuracy of recording, but does not necessarily prove that amounts were entered in the correct account, nor would it disclose that a transaction had been omitted from both account entries.

The 'T' accounts are not seen as such in computerized accounting, but the basic principle of debit and credit is still observed. Accounting software is available to do all the double entry bookkeeping, extract the trial balance, and go on to produce the income statement and balance sheet.

As managers, our interest in bookkeeping has not been for its own sake but as an explanation of why a balance sheet must always balance, and where all the information comes from to produce the monthly and annual accounts. This can be shown diagrammatically in Figure 1.1.

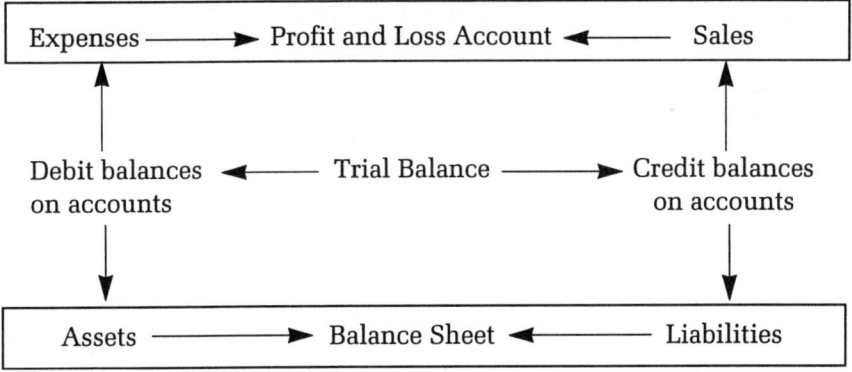

Figure 1.1 *Trial balance leading to the final accounts*

Let us now take the example of a trial balance shown in Figure 1.2 relating to a market trader and produce a profit and loss account and balance sheet, as in Figure 1.3. Profit is derived from the difference between sales and expenses, but to keep the double entry principle going we will show the second entry of profit as an increase in the business owner's capital. This is of course true if the owner retains all the profit made in the business and does not distribute it in the form of a cash dividend.

Trial balance

Debit balances:	£	Credit balances:	£
Cash a/c	400	Capital a/c	500
Purchases a/c	4000	A Supplier a/c (creditor)	200
Wages a/c	1300	Sales a/c	8200
Rent a/c	1000		
Equipment a/c	1500		
A Customer a/c (debtor)	700		
	£8900		£8900

Figure 1.2 *Trial balance of a market trader*

Profit and loss account

Expenses:	£	Revenues:	£
Purchases	4000	Sales	8200
Wages	1300		
Rent	1000		
Total expenses	6300		
Profit (£8200–£6300)	1900		
	£8200		£8200

Balance sheet

Assets:	£	Liabilities:	£
Equipment	1500	Original capital	500
Debtors (A Customer)	700	Retained profit	1900
Cash	400		
		Total capital	2400
		Creditor (A Supplier)	200
	£2600		£2600

Figure 1.3 *Profit and loss account and balance sheet*

No matter how large the organization these principles still apply, although more detailed breakdowns of expenses, assets, sales and liabilities will result in more complex statements than those shown here.

At the end of each accounting period, accountants make adjustments for prepayments and accruals of sales revenue and expenses to ensure that the matching convention is preserved.

A 'prepayment' occurs when an expense or asset is paid for by a business before it is received. A typical example might be rent if it is paid quarterly in advance. At the end of the first month, two months' rent is prepaid, while at the end of the second month one month's rent is prepaid. Such prepayments are an asset to the business and are recorded in debtors in the balance sheet, while the rent account is reduced to what relates to that period only.

Customers can also prepay by making deposits or payments in advance. These are shown as creditors in the balance sheet statement until value is given and the sale completed.

An 'accrual' occurs where any expenditure is incurred but no invoice has yet been received when accountants close off the books at month-ends. An estimate of the amount is included in the expense/asset account with the double entry showing accruals as part of creditors in the balance sheet. 'Accrued income' is also possible for items such as interest earned but not yet received.

Some organizations will also need to consolidate the accounts of smaller business units. *Group* or *consolidated accounts* combine the accounts of all businesses under the control of a parent organization to give a combined picture of trading performance and financial position as though they were all one entity. You may be familiar with this legal requirement already if you work for a company that forms part of a larger group.

We look at the details of the profit and loss account and balance sheet in the following chapters, but first we will take stock of what we have covered so far.

SUMMARY

Financial reporting by organizations is concentrated on three key accounting statements. The profit and loss account and cash flow statements have recently been altered in format by FRS 3 and FRS 1 respectively. The balance sheet is also under scrutiny at the moment and a new standard is expected. The changes that have been introduced are aimed at making these statements more meaningful and less amenable to 'creative accounting'.

Information going into all financial statements is the result of detailed financial recording of all cash and credit transactions when they occur. As we will see later, managers like yourself have a part to play in ensuring that account codes are correctly entered on accounting documents passing through your hands, and that accruals are identified at each month end.

References

1. Accounting Standards Committee (1975) The Corporate Report, Discussion Paper.
2. Cadbury Committee (1992) *Financial aspects of corporate governance*, Professional Publishing Ltd, London.
3. Kirk, R (1993) 'Accounting standards: the pace of change accelerates', *Management Accounting* (UK), December.
4. Lawrence, S C (1992) 'The diversity of accounting in a single Europe', *Management Accounting* (UK), March.
5. Cairns, D (1993) 'The IASC—20 more years of vision and commitment', *Accountancy*, July.

2

The income statement

An income statement measures financial performance during a discrete period of time, for example a month or a year, by comparing the sales generated with the expenditure incurred in that same period. The resulting surplus or deficit is a measure of the organization's financial performance, particularly in the case of profit-seeking enterprises. Non-profit-seeking organizations should try to live within their means, so the surplus or deficit on an income statement is also an indicator of their financial performance.

TYPES OF INCOME STATEMENT

Income statements come in three forms, and you will be able to identify your own from the following descriptions:

- *Profit and loss account*—the form used by all limited companies and other trading organizations where the profit motive is evident.
- *Revenue account*—applies to local authorities and some public bodies.
- *Income and expenditure account*—used by voluntary organizations where the profit motive is absent, for example charities or societies. This statement is the same as a profit and loss account except for tax and dividends which are not relevant.

All three statements compare income earned in the period with the expenses consumed in the same period, and broadly follow the same accounting principles. One difference between the three income statements relates to their sources of revenue. For example, a local authority will have rates, council tax and government grants as its main sources of income in its revenue account. Any charges for services rendered will be a minor source of revenue to a local authority, but in profit-seeking enterprises sales of goods and services will be the main source of revenue.

The other main difference between the types of income statement relates to what happens to any surplus or deficit. In the local authority any surplus or deficit is carried forward to the following year. A surplus reduces the burden on ratepayers in the following year; a deficit has the opposite effect.

With profit-seeking companies the destination of profits or losses is different. Profits attract corporation tax, which for larger companies is at the rate of 33 per cent. Any profit after tax results in an increase in the value of the shareholders' funds. When cash dividends are paid, this reduces the asset, cash, and reduces the shareholders' funds by an identical amount.

Government accounting is moving closer to private sector accounting and local authorities are involved in *compulsory competitive tendering* and the preparation of trading accounts. It would therefore seem that a concentration on profit and loss accounts and their fundamental principles will be appropriate to most readers.

PROFIT AND LOSS ACCOUNT

We now need to examine exactly what is meant by a profit or a loss. The metaphorical 'man in the street' would probably say that profit is the difference between the sales price and the purchase price of something. As we shall see from the next example, even this definition is not so straightforward!

Example

You decide to start trading and buy some stock for £3000, of which you pay £2000 immediately and manage to get the remaining £1000 on credit. By the end of the month you have sold half your stock for £3600, of which you have received £3300 and the remaining £300 you expect to receive shortly. You are confident you can sell the remaining half of your original stock next month. How much profit have you made in this first month?

A profit and loss account is a summary of a firm's sales or revenues offset by the cost of the goods or services sold and other running costs. The method and timing of payments to and by the firm is irrelevant to the profit and loss account, but not of course to the balance sheet, as we shall see later. The cost of the goods sold is £1500 which, taken from the sales value of £3600, leaves a gross profit of £2100.

Gross profit is the term used to describe the profit level after the cost of sales but before the overhead expenses are deducted. *Net profit* results after all overheads are deducted from the gross profit. The basic structure of a profit and loss account is shown in Figure 2.1.

	£m
Sales	100
Cost of sales	60
Gross profit	40
Overheads	25
Net profit	15

Figure 2.1 *Basic structure of a profit and loss account*

There are two tests of whether or not a cost goes into the profit and loss account as opposed to the balance sheet. First, the cost of sales must relate to sales of goods and services included in the same statement. Second, in the case of overhead expenses, these must relate to the exact time period covered by the statement. The sum of the cost of sales and overheads as defined here is referred to as *revenue expenditure.*

It is a common misconception that the profit and loss account is a summary of all cash flowing into and out of the business, and that the excess of cash receipts over cash payments represents the profit. Such thinking ignores the reality that long-life expenditure on assets or any loans taken out goes in the balance sheet, not the profit and loss account.

In today's world most transactions are on credit, and the cash receipts and payments in one month usually reflect transactions that occurred in a previous month(s), not transactions going in this month's profit and loss account. An exception is wage and salary payments which are mainly made in the same month that their cost goes in the profit and loss account.

STOCKS

When goods are manufactured or purchased for resale, they are rarely all sold in the same month, so giving rise to stocks at month-ends and the year-end. A basic principle of the profit and loss account is that sales must be matched with the cost of those same sales, and not with the cost of purchases.

With ongoing companies we therefore have two stock figures to contend with—the opening stock at the beginning of the period and the closing stock at the end of the period. Opening stock is brought forward from a previous period, while closing stock is deducted from this period and carried forward to the next period. These adjustments for changing stock levels are shown in the *trading account* section of the profit and loss account.

Example

A retail firm sold goods for £50,000 one month when purchases cost £30,000. Stock brought forward from the previous month was £12,000, which had increased to £15,000 by this month's end. The cost of sales is shown as £27,000 in the trading account, as calculated in Figure 2.2.

	£	£
Sales		50,000
Purchases	30,000	
Add: Opening stock	12,000	
	42,000	
Less: Closing stock	15,000	
Cost of sales		27,000
Gross profit		£23,000

Figure 2.2 *Trading account showing treatment of stocks*

Manufacturing companies will not just have stocks of finished goods, as they usually hold stocks of raw materials and may have partly finished goods called 'work in progress'. Opening and closing stocks of these items are adjusted in a similar way to that illustrated in Figure 2.2 when calculating manufacturing costs for a period.

DEPRECIATION

Cash can be spent by a firm in two ways. Either cash is spent on goods and services that are consumed immediately, for example salaries, materials and overheads, or it is spent on fixed assets with a life expectancy of some years, for example buildings and equipment.

The only real difference between the two for accountancy purposes is the life span, which is crucially important when we try to measure financial performance over short discrete periods of one month or one year. Although it is right to charge the cost of salaries, materials and overheads to the month in which they were consumed, it would be grossly unfair to charge the full purchase cost of a fixed asset like a building against only one month's revenue. This is why accountants distinguish between revenue expenditure and capital expenditure.

This problem is overcome by charging a proportion of the cost of fixed assets, called 'depreciation', in each monthly profit and loss account.

Example

A machine costs £60,000 to buy and is expected to last five years. This would result in a depreciation charge of £1000 in each monthly profit and loss account for the next five years. If the life span turns out to be longer, then no further depreciation is charged after five years; if shorter, then extra depreciation has to be charged in the last month of the asset's life.

This approach is one of the two main methods of depreciation used in the UK, with a third being used in the USA. These three are called:

- straight line method;
- reducing balance method;
- sum-of-the-digits method.

Straight line method

As described in the above example, the straight line method charges an equal amount of depreciation each year over the expected life of the asset. In some cases a residual value might be expected, in which case the calculation is varied slightly so that the depreciated value of the asset falls to the expected residual value after its period of use with the firm.

Example

Taking the earlier machine with an original cost of £60,000, we will now assume that it has an expected residual value of £10,000 at the end of five years. This requires only £50,000 to be written off as depreciation over this time, resulting in a depreciation charge of £10,000 each year.

$$Annual\ depreciation = \frac{original\ cost - residual\ value}{estimated\ life}$$

$$= \frac{£60,000 - £10,000}{5} = £10,000\ per\ annum$$

Reducing balance method

The reducing balance method takes a very different approach to the straight line method. Instead of charging a constant amount of depreciation in each time period, a constant percentage is charged on the reducing value of the asset, so resulting in a lower depreciation charge as each year goes by. The percentage to use is found from the formula:

$$r = 100 - \left(\sqrt[n]{\frac{\text{residual value}}{\text{original cost}}} \times 100 \right)$$

where n equals the estimated life in years and r equals the depreciation rate. Using the same example, we can solve the equation:

$$r = 100 - \left(\sqrt[5]{\frac{\text{residual value}}{\text{original cost}}} \times 100 \right)$$

$$r = 30\% \text{ approx}$$

This method results in a depreciation charge of £18,000 in the first year, falling by 30 per cent each year to £12,600 in the second year and £8820 in the third year, resulting in a rapid fall in the value of the asset under this type of depreciation to £20,580 at the end of the third year. This compares with a written down value of £30,000 after three years under the straight line method.

Sum-of-the-digits method

The sum-of-the-sigits method is a form of reducing balance method, but the decline in yearly depreciation charges is less severe. The digits represent the figures for each year of the life of the asset, so the sum is all the years' figures added together. Depreciation in any one year is the fraction of that year over the sum of all the years.

In the UK, both the straight line and reducing balance methods are

Example

In the five-year life example, the sum of the digits is:
5 + 4 + 3 + 2 + 1 = 15. The first year's depreciation charge will be the fraction 5/15, the second year's 4/15, and the third year's 3/15 of the amount to be depreciated over the five years. If £50,000 is to be written off over five years then depreciation starts at £16,667 for the first year, reduces to £13,333 for the second year, £10,000 for the third year and so on.

accepted by the accounting profession, but the reducing balance method is not normally used to depreciate buildings or leases. Either method can be used on plant, equipment and vehicles, but it is on motor cars that the reducing balance method is most commonly seen.

TAXATION

The Inland Revenue is not interested in depreciation charged by a company, regardless of which method is used. This is because they have their own system of tax allowances which substitute for depreciation.

Corporation tax is the system of taxation which applies to the profits of all limited companies, as opposed to income tax which applies to profits of the self-employed and partnerships. Differences between the two systems are mainly confined to the rates of tax and the timing of tax payments. We concentrate here on the taxation of limited company profits.

There is one standard rate of corporation tax, set at 33 per cent at the time of writing. This applies to all companies with taxable profits in excess of £1.5m. Below this profit figure, the tax rate decreases on a tapering basis down to the standard rate of income tax, so that a small business is not disadvantaged by incorporation.

The profit on which corporation tax is levied is not identical with the profit disclosed in the firm's profit and loss account, but is an adjusted figure after some costs have been disallowed and capital allowances substituted for the company's own depreciation. For this reason, it is never possible for a company to manipulate its tax charge by altering its depreciation policy. The Inland Revenue will add back whatever depreciation a company charges in its profit and loss account. Figure 2.3 shows the main adjustments that take place.

		£
Profit as shown in the profit and loss account		4,040,000
Add back disallowed expenses:		
Depreciation	200,000	
Entertainment	10,000	
Political contributions	6,000	216,000
		4,256,000
Deduct:		
Capital allowances		(256,000)
Taxable profit		£4,000,000
Corporation tax payable is £4.0m × 33% = £1,320,000		

Figure 2.3 *Corporation tax assessment*

The capital allowances for all firms in all industries are based on two systems applied to different assets. The size of these allowances varies from time to time, as they are used by the Chancellor of the Exchequer to help regulate economic activity. The current allowances are:

| Industrial buildings | 4 per cent per annum on a straight line basis for 25 years |
| Plant, equipment, furniture and motor vehicles | 25 per cent per annum on a reducing balance basis |

One result of the difference between tax allowances and depreciation is that companies often appear to be paying less than the standard rate of corporation tax on their profits, as is the case in Figure 2.4. This occurs when the tax allowances exceed the depreciation charge in any one year. This could ultimately be reversed if a company slowed down its capital expenditure such that depreciation on old assets exceeded the tax allowances, then not so heavily influenced by recent capital expenditure.

If that situation is expected to arise in the not-too-distant future, a provision is made by charging the extra tax in the profit and loss account now. The current tax that has to be paid is shown as a short-term creditor until the time of payment, while the *provision for deferred taxation* is shown with other provisions and charges as a long-term liability in the balance sheet. In this way companies avoid their tax charge exceeding 33 per cent of their profit because of the difference between tax allowances and depreciation. The provision is reduced in the future when it is needed to keep the tax charge down to 33 per cent.

LAYOUT OF A PROFIT AND LOSS ACCOUNT

We can now look at a fuller version of the profit and loss account in Figure 2.4, suitable for a trading organization.

Strictly speaking, what we are calling the profit and loss account comprises three or four different sections which companies select as appropriate to their business. Only the last three of the possible four sections shown below apply in the example in Figure 2.4.

- *Section 1* Manufacturing account—shows the cost of any goods manufactured.
- *Section 2* Trading account—matches cost of sales against sales to derive gross profit.

	£000
Sales	50,000
Cost of sales	(27,000)
Gross profit	23,000
Wages and salaries	(7,500)
Directors fees	(2,500)
National Insurance and pension contributions	(2,300)
Rent and business rates	(3,500)
Depreciation	(1,400)
Electricity, gas etc	(700)
Stationery, postage, telephone	(650)
Vehicle running expenses	(2,500)
Auditors' fees and other professional charges	(200)
Bank interest and charges	(360)
Net profit before tax	1,390
Taxation	(410)
Net profit after taxation	980
Dividends	(520)
Retained profit	460

Note: The convention of bracketed figures is used to denote a deduction.

Figure 2.4 *Profit and loss account for internal use*

■ *Section 3* Profit and loss account—deducts overhead expenses to derive net profit after taxation.
■ *Section 4* Appropriation account—shows the dividends and profit retained.

Published profit and loss accounts

A published profit and loss account does not usually disclose the degree of detail shown in Figure 2.4 about expenses. Only some of the items are obliged to be disclosed by law, and for reasons of confidentiality companies do not normally make public more detail than is required.

Very often, expenses are grouped together under a few headings, with the mandatory details being left to the detailed notes accompanying the main statements, rather than forming part of them. This allows the reader to see the broad impact without being swamped in a morass of figures. One of the formats for reporting financial performance approved by the 1985 Companies Act is shown in Figure 2.5 for Northern Electric plc.[1]

Group profit and loss account for the year ended 31 March 1993

	1993 £m	1992 £m
Turnover	882.7	813.7
Cost of sales	(611.1)	(552.4)
Gross profit	271.6	261.3
Distribution costs	(74.6)	(78.7)
Administrative expenses	(92.1)	(86.4)
Other operating income	1.5	1.3
Operating profit	106.4	97.5
Income from investments	10.7	10.2
Profit on ordinary activities before interest	117.1	107.7
Net interest	(5.7)	(9.5)
Profit on ordinary activities before taxation	111.4	98.2
Tax on profit on ordinary activities	(26.1)	(24.9)
Profit attributable to members of the parent company	85.3	73.3
Dividends	(26.4)	(22.8)
Retained profit for the year	58.9	50.5
	pence	*pence*
Earnings per share—basic	69.3	59.6

Statement of recognized gains and losses

There are no recognised gains or losses other than £85.3m profit attributable to shareholders of the company in the year ended 31 March 1993 and £73.3m in the year ended 31 March 1992.

Figure 2.5 *Published group profit and loss account for Northern Electric plc*

Commentary

It might be useful at this stage to relate some of the accounting principles and conventions mentioned earlier to Northern Electric's 1993 profit and loss account.

- *Historical cost accounting (HCA)*—The accounts are prepared under the HCA convention and in accordance with applicable standards.
- *Turnover*—another word for sales or revenues. The figure of £882.7m includes the sales value of goods and services provided and all electricity consumed during the year.

- *VAT*—this is not included in any figures in the accounting statements, except for the amount owing to or by the Customs and Excise which is shown as a creditor or debtor respectively in the balance sheet.
- *Cost of sales*—this is based on accrual accounting so that the costs of goods, services and electricity supplied to customers in the year relates to the same items included as turnover.
- *Distribution and administrative costs*—these include staff costs, depreciation, hire costs and other overheads.
- *Income from investments*—this all relates to a dividend and associated tax credit receivable from an investment in National Grid Holding plc, which is owned collectively by the 12 regional electricity companies.
- *Interest*—the net amount shown of £5.7m is the difference between interest payable of £9.1m and interest receivable of £3.4m.
- *Tax*—the tax charge of £26.1m is significantly affected by timing differences of capital allowances in excess of depreciation.
- *Dividends*—the £26.4m represents the interim dividend already paid and the final dividend payable after the annual general meeting has approved its declaration. Companies tend to keep their dividend payments in line with the trend in profits in the long run.
- *Profit*—this is presented at seven different levels to allow readers to monitor progress at those levels. More and more items are included as we progress down the statement. The seven levels at which profit is disclosed are:

1. gross profit;
2. operating profit;
3. profit before interest;
4. profit before tax;
5. profit attributable to members of the parent company;
6. retained profit for the year;
7. earnings per share.

The profit attributable to members of the parent company is the profit level used to calculate the earnings per share, which is regarded by many as the 'bottom line'. When dividends paid and payable are deducted from the attributable profit, we find the amount of profit retained in the business during the year. In effect, the shareholders' interest in the net assets of the company has increased by £58.9m. This shows as an increase under the capital and reserves heading in the group balance sheet, which is illustrated in the next chapter.

In Chapter 5 we return to discuss how some of these profit measures are used in the calculation of accounting ratios and performance measures. Examples are 'profit margins' and 'return on capital employed'. First, we need to examine the make-up of the balance sheet as there are interconnections between the two statements.

SUMMARY

If you look at any published profit and loss account or income statement, you will see the latest year's figures alongside those for the previous year. You can get a quick grasp of whether things have got better or worse by looking at the absolute change in value of sales, profit and each cost item.

Further insight can be gained by calculating the percentage change for each item from the previous year. For example, if sales have gone up 10 per cent and the cost of sales is up 7 per cent for a retail organization, this tells us that either selling prices have improved, or better purchase prices were obtained. Try examining your own organization's income statement and judge whether or not its financial performance has improved.

Finally, as we shall see in Chapter 6, there have been changes to published profit and loss accounts for accounting years ending after 22 June 1993. The new standard FRS 3, entitled *Reporting financial performance*,[2] aims to make the profit and loss account more meaningful and less capable of manipulation by creative accounting. Of necessity, the standard makes the account more comprehensive and therefore harder to read and understand.

References

1. Northern Electric plc (1993) *Annual report and accounts*, Newcastle upon Tyne.
2. The Accounting Standards Board Ltd (1992) FRS 3: *Reporting financial performance*.

3

The balance sheet

A balance sheet is a financial photograph of a business at a single point in time, usually the last day of a month or the last day of the year. On the one hand it shows the value of all the assets (possessions) owned by the business, and on the other it shows the sources of funds with which those assets were acquired.

Here we have an example of the dual aspect of double entry book-keeping where assets are matched by equal values of liabilities. This is why a balance sheet must always balance in the sense that:

Balance sheet

Assets   =   *Liabilities*

This balance sheet equation can best be understood by showing a few simple examples of transactions that involve both assets and liabilities.

Example 1

A N Other starts up a business by paying £1000 into a newly opened business bank account. The balance sheet for the business now reflects the asset of £1000 cash and the liability of the business to repay the owner who provided that amount of capital, as follows:

<u>A N Other's balance sheet</u>

Assets:	£	Liabilities:	£
Cash	1000	Owner's capital	1000

Example 2

If some cash is now spent on the purchase of £400 stock, there is no change in the balance sheet totals but there is a change in the composition of the total assets. Some cash has been exchanged for a different asset, namely stock, as follows:

A N Other's balance sheet

Assets:	£	Liabilities:	£
Stock	400	Owner's capital	1000
Cash	600		
	1000		1000

Example 3

Further stock costing £200 is now bought on credit from A Supplier. The asset, stock, increases by this amount, as do liabilities with the introduction of *creditors*, being the amount owing to suppliers, as follows:

A N Other's Balance sheet

Assets:	£	Liabilities:	£
Stock (400 + 200)	600	Owner's capital	1000
Cash	600	Creditors	200
	1200		1200

Example 4

Some stock which originally cost £100 is now sold for cash of £150, thereby making a profit of £50. This shows partly as a switch from the asset of stock to cash and also as an increase in total assets to £1250. The profit of £50 is a further claim by the owner on the business and effectively increases the owner's capital, as follows:

A N Other's balance sheet

Assets:	£	Liabilities:	£
Stock (600 − 100)	500	Owner's capital (1000 + 50)	1050
Cash (600 + 150)	750	Creditors	200
	1250		1250

Having justified why a balance sheet must always balance, let us return to examine this statement in more detail. Assets come in two main types known as *fixed assets* and *current assets*. Fixed assets are the hardware, the physical things the business uses itself which are not for sale to customers. Your own organization will have some of the following examples of fixed assets: land, buildings, plant, equipment, furniture and vehicles.

Current assets are in the process of being turned into cash and include stocks, work in progress, trade debtors (amounts due from customers) and cash and bank balances. Therefore we can say:

Total assets = Fixed assets + Current assets

Shareholders provide funds to finance the company's acquisition of fixed and current assets when they buy shares issued directly by that company. This share capital is augmented by any profits retained in the business as opposed to all the profit being paid in the form of dividends. The technical term for retained profit is *reserves*, which can also arise in other ways. The total of *share capital plus reserves* represents the interest of the shareholders in the *net assets* of the company.

Further funds can be obtained by a company from borrowings, either on a short-term overdraft basis or by short-term and/or long-term loans. The final source of finance is obtained through credit normally granted by suppliers.

Total liabilities = Share capital + reserves + borrowings + other creditors

The same equation holds true for all organizations except that share capital does not exist for local authorities and charities. In their case, capital is either borrowed or is the accumulation of surpluses (less deficits) since they came into existence.

Having identified the main components of a company balance sheet, we can draw the total picture, first keeping to the balance sheet equation that total assets equal total liabilities, as in Figure 3.1.

Balance Sheet

Assets:	£m	Liabilities:	£m
Fixed assets	100	Share capital and reserves	200
		Creditors due after one year	50
Current assets	250	Creditors due within one year	100
Total assets	350	Total liabilities	350

Figure 3.1 *Balance sheet outline in horizontal format*

The style of horizontal presentation shown in Figure 3.1 is rarely used and the required layout laid down by law and the relevant accounting standards uses the vertical presentation in Figure 3.2, which you will see in your own organization's accounts.

Balance sheet		
	£m	£m
Fixed assets		100
Current assets	250	
Creditors falling due within one year	(100)	
Net current assets or working capital		150
Total assets less current liabilities		250
Creditors falling due after one year		(50)
Net assets attributable to the shareholders		200
Share capital and reserves		200

Figure 3.2 *Balance sheet outline in vertical format*

Note: Total assets less current liabilities (£250m) if often referred to as capital employed.

FIXED ASSETS

Fixed assets are grouped under three possible subheadings, although they may not all be required in some organizations:

- tangible fixed assets;
- intangible fixed assets;
- investments.

Tangible fixed assets

Tangible fixed assets are assets held in the business for use over the years rather than for resale. They include land and buildings, plant and machinery, motor vehicles and furniture and fittings.

They are normally shown in a balance sheet at their original cost less the accumulated depreciation. This written down value, or *book value*, may not represent the saleable value at that time, partly because of inflation, but also because a forced sale does not necessarily bring full value. In a sense, the book value represents the unexpired value remaining to the company.

The practice of depreciating fixed assets is extended to some leased assets. Here a distinction needs to be made between *operating leases* and *finance leases*. The former represents the hire of a piece of plant or a vehicle for a short time, eg days, weeks or a month or two, after which the item is simply returned to the hire company. These operating lease charges or hire charges are charged to the profit and loss account when they are incurred. The asset or assets concerned do not appear in the balance sheet.

A *finance lease* is more akin to hire purchase without the purchase option at the end. It is a long-term contract to hire a vehicle or a piece of equipment (or in fact any fixed asset). The full capital value of the leased asset is shown in the balance sheet with the finance debt or obligation to the lessor split between short-term and long-term creditors. The asset value is then depreciated each year by the amount of the capital repayments made during the year. Interest charges on the lease agreement are also included in the profit and loss account as they are incurred.

The task of keeping track of all fixed assets, together with their associated depreciation charges and tax allowances over their whole life, is a mammoth one. Larger organizations, your own possibly included, make use of information technology for this purpose. Accounting packages dedicated to keeping an *asset register* are widely available.

Intangible fixed assets

The category of intangible fixed assets embraces:

- *Goodwill*—the name and reputation of a company that bring customers back, eg Marks and Spencer. Such goodwill is built up over many years but can also be purchased if another company is acquired. Goodwill in this case is the difference between the amount paid for the company and its net assets as shown in the balance sheet.
- *Brands*—somewhat akin to goodwill but specifically relating to the value of a brand name built up over the years, primarily by advertising a good quality product, eg Guinness or Mars bars.
- *Patent*—a legal monopoly over the specific design of a product or service.

Such items only tend to appear in the balance sheet if they are separately identifiable and cash has been spent on their acquisition. Goodwill and brands are very contentious items at present and are the subject of much debate both within the accounting profession and by the top management of quoted companies.

When a company pays more to acquire a company than the fair value of its tangible assets, the difference is usually referred to as goodwill. Accounting policy in the UK, but not in all other countries, is that such goodwill is usually written off against retained profit or reserves at the time of acquisition. This puts acquired goodwill on the same footing as internally generated goodwill, which does not generally appear on the balance sheet because its cost cannot be separately identified.

The alternative accounting policy in the UK is to put acquired goodwill in the balance sheet and to depreciate it through the profit and loss account each year. This reduces the profit and the all-important earnings per share, so it is little wonder that, given a choice, few companies opt for this approach. The alternative of writing goodwill off against reserves has no impact on future profits and earnings per share, but is reflected in a reduced capital and reserves figure in the balance sheet.

Some companies have jumped the gun, anticipating a change in the relevant accounting standards, and have brought *brand values* onto their balance sheets. Arguably brand values are part of a company's goodwill. The basis for valuing brands and goodwill is discussed in Chapter 6, along with other developments and contentious topics.

Investments

The category of investments is one of very few that can appear under both fixed and current asset headings. Investments only appear as a fixed asset if they are long term in nature and represent a stake in a subsidiary, a joint venture or an associated company. A subsidiary is one where more than 50 per cent of the voting shares are held, whereas an associate is one where a minority holding is held of a substantial amount, for example more than 20 per cent of the equity. An equity holding of less than 20 per cent is called a trade investment.

CURRENT ASSETS

Current assets are short-term assets which are already cash, or which are intended to be turned back into cash in the course of normal trading activity, and within 12 months of the balance sheet date. They include:

- stocks of raw material;
- work in progress;
- stocks of finished goods;
- debtors;
- short-term investments;
- cash and bank balances.

Stocks

It is possible to have up to three types of stocks, depending on the nature of the business. A manufacturing company will have raw materials, work in progress and finished goods, whereas a retail company will only have finished goods or goods for resale. If you work for a service organization stocks may be unimportant, but many such companies have considerable work in progress, or stocks of consumable items. For example, an architect will have incurred labour and overhead costs on drawings not yet charged out to clients. These costs represent work in progress.

Stocks are valued at their original cost, or realizable value if that happens to be less than the cost.

If you work for a company that holds large stocks of commodities, you may be familiar with the effect of this rule on your company's stock values and profits at year-ends, when results are reported to shareholders. Oil, basic metals, cocoa, sugar, rubber, are all examples of commodities that may fluctuate in price and hence affect stock values.

If the market value of a commodity happens to be lower than the original purchase cost, this results in a stock loss and a fall in profits. Oil companies are particularly vulnerable to this rule, which can of course work in reverse.

The valuation of work in progress and finished goods may also not be quite as straightforward as *valuing at cost* would suggest. Obviously the direct costs of labour and materials going into the product or service are part of the cost. So too is a share of the productive overheads, but not selling, administration and distribution overheads. Fortunately, some rules have been formulated by the profession and these are found in the accountancy standard SSAP 9.

The value of stocks held in store is also influenced by the stores' pricing policy, which may value them at an *average cost*, at a *standard cost* or on a *first-in-first-out* basis. This topic is explained more fully in Chapter 7 on costing.

Debtors

Any party who owes money to a company is called a debtor, of which the most important category is trade debtors, being customers who have been invoiced for credit sales and who have not yet paid. Apart from retail organizations, you should expect to see trade debtors in all company balance sheets. Also included under debtors are any prepayments made by the company in advance of the goods or services being received, for example rent paid for the month following the date of the balance sheet.

The basis for valuing trade debtors is to take the value of all the customer invoices outstanding and deduct a small provision for possible bad debts. Such a provision is based on past experience and a knowledge of the current economic climate. This provision is charged as an expense in the profit and loss account and needs adjusting periodically in the light of actual bad debts.

Investments, cash and bank balances

When an organization has funds surplus to its needs, it may invest them in short-term investments like government stocks or other securities, for which the market value should be disclosed. These investments are very different in nature to the long-term investments included in fixed assets.

All businesses have a current account, possibly a deposit account, and where large sums are involved they may make deposits overnight on the money markets. The treasury function ensures that the best return is achieved on short-term bank deposits.

BALANCE SHEET SEQUENCE

The groups of assets mentioned below are normally listed in order of their permanence, as illustrated in Figure 3.3.

Fixed assets
Tangible fixed assets:
       Land and buildings
       Plant and machinery
       Motor vehicles
       Furniture and fittings
Intangible fixed assets:
       Patents and trade marks
       Goodwill
Investments:
       Interest in associated company

Current assets
Stocks:
       Raw materials
       Work in progress
       Finished goods
Debtors
Investments
Cash and bank balances

Figure 3.3 *Sequence of balance sheet assets*

SOURCES OF FUNDS

We now turn our attention to a business's source of funds—where the finance came from with which the assets were acquired. In the case of a limited company, the two main sources are shareholders and borrowings from financial institutions.

An additional source of finance is business trade credit when purchases of goods and services are settled some weeks after their receipt, according to the particular terms of business. To these trade creditors must be added tax and dividends, which are always paid a number of months after the end of the financial year to which they relate. Unlike shareholders' funds and borrowings, these are 'free' sources of finance to a company, in the sense that an interest cost is not attached to them.

Share capital

Ordinary shares are the risk or equity capital of every company. Ordinary shares have no fixed dividend rate, so dividend distributions usually follow the trend of profits. Only part of the profit for the financial year is normally paid out in the form of dividends; the remainder, or retained profit is added to the reserves mentioned below.

Preference shares normally do have a fixed rate of dividend and have priority over ordinary shares, for both dividend payments and any repayment of capital.

Issued share capital is the value of shares that have been issued at their nominal or par value. Any sale of shares for more than this value is entered as a reserve. This is what normally happens on a *rights issue* when new shares are sold to shareholders at a discount to their current value. The nominal value received goes in the balance sheet as *issued share capital*. The difference between the price at which new shares are sold and their nominal or par value is called a *share premium* and goes in the reserves. This is balanced by the total cash received from the sale of shares which goes in the bank account.

Example

A company issues 2m new shares of 50p nominal value at a price of £1.50. Ignoring issue costs, assets increase by the £3m received in cash. Share capital increases by £1m and the reserves increase by £2m (in respect of the share premium of £1 per share).

A very different type of share issue goes by the name of a 'scrip issue', which is a free issue of shares. In effect, it turns reserves into permanent issued share capital. This merely takes a sum from one line of the balance sheet and places it on the next. It brings no new cash into the company and gives shareholders nothing they do not already own. If the scrip issue was a 'one for one' issue, the value of both old and new shares would be half what the original shares were worth before the issue.

Reserves

'Reserves' is probably one of the most misleading terms in accounting. In general, it means all the profits that have been retained in the company. Examples are:

■ retained profits, less losses, from each year's profit and loss account;
■ share premium account—the excess over the par value when new shares are sold;
■ revaluation reserves—the increase in value of any assets, notably land and buildings, caused mainly by inflation.

Creditors falling due after one year

Creditors falling due after one year come under two main categories—borrowings and provisions. Borrowings at a fixed rate of interest are attractive to a company, as it obtains tax relief on the interest and pays less for the capital than it can usually earn in the business. If borrowings are kept modest relative to the amount of share capital and reserves, referred to as 'low gearing', then the risk factor is reduced.

Sometimes companies make provisions for losses expected from future events, say a restructuring programme. A provision is made by charging an estimate of this cost, called a provision, in the profit and loss account now. At a later date, the actual costs are charged against this provision and then any excess charges to subsequent profit and loss accounts. Should the provision exceed the actual costs incurred, then an adjustment to profit will be shown in a future profit and loss account.

Creditors falling due within one year

Creditors falling due within one year are amounts owing by the company that need paying within twelve months of the date of the balance sheet. Typical items are:

■ bank overdrafts;
■ other borrowings due within one year;

- trade creditors;
- corporation tax;
- PAYE/National Insurance not yet paid;
- VAT owing to Customs and Excise.

Creditors falling due within one year is also called current liabilities.

Working capital

It is customary to show the creditors falling due within one year as a deduction from the current assets which they help to finance. This arrives at what is termed *net current assets* in a balance sheet, more familiarly known as *working capital*.

Current assets - Creditors due within one year = Working capital

The calculation of working capital implies that short-term creditors finance some of the current assets and only the net current assets require financing by long-term borrowings and shareholders funds.

Other sources of finance

There are various other forms of finance that are neither pure shares nor pure borrowings, and which sometimes change in nature in the future. Among these are:

- convertible loan or debenture;
- convertible preference share;
- mezzanine loan, as sometimes found in a management buy-out;
- sale and leaseback of a building;
- invoice discounting or factoring.

When deciding on their sources of funds, companies have to consider such factors as availability, cost, risk, repayment burden and so on.

The sources of finance follow on from the assets in a vertical presentation of a balance sheet, but the sequence of the items in terms of their permanence is reversed. Short-term creditors are deducted from current assets to derive the working capital, to which is added the fixed assets to derive the value of *total assets less current liabilities.*

Long-term creditors and any provisions for liabilities and charges are now deducted from total assets less current liabilities, to give the value of *net assets.* These are shown as financed by the share capital and reserves.

We can now look at a complete balance sheet in the usual vertical format, incorporating most of the items we have discussed. The example chosen in Figure 3.4 is the Northern Electric plc group balance sheet as at 31 March 1993.[1] This is used in a later chapter, together with the group profit and loss account, to illustrate accounting ratios.

Group balance sheet as at 31 March 1993

	1993 £m	1992 £m
Fixed assets		
Tangible assets	361.5	333.2
Investments	88.0	53.4
	449.5	386.6
Current assets		
Stocks	9.5	10.6
Debtors	169.3	157.9
Investments	26.1	10.4
Cash at bank and in hand	9.0	4.4
	213.9	183.3
Creditors: amounts falling due within one year	(131.9)	(120.4)
Net current assets (working capital)	82.0	62.9
Total assets less current liabilities	531.5	449.5
Creditors:		
amounts falling due after more than one year	(62.6)	(57.0)
Provisions for liabilities and charges	(44.2)	(26.8)
Total assets less liabilities (net assets)	424.7	365.7
Capital and reserves		
Called up share capital	61.6	61.5
Reserves	363.1	304.2
	424.7	365.7

Figure 3.4 *Published group balance sheet for Northern Electric plc*

Commentary

The Northern Electric plc group balance sheet illustrated in Figure 3.4 is prepared under the historical cost accounting convention. We return to discuss this aspect and an alternative presentation under the current cost accounting convention in Chapter 6.

Significant changes in balance sheet items compared to the previous year are:

■ *Fixed assets*—capital expenditure on tangible fixed assets of £63.5m reduced to a net increase in book value of £28.3m after depreciation and consumers' contributions were taken into account. Investments increased by £34.6m, of which £31.3m went on a shareholding in a gas-fired power station and £3.3m in a company planning a new national telephone system.

■ *Current assets*—short-term investments and cash balances increased by £20.8m, which is the amount shown in the group cash flow statement as the increase in *cash and cash equivalents*. This statement is discussed in the following chapter.

■ *Provisions*—the increase of £17.4m is mainly the regulatory correction factor caused by an overrecovery of revenue compared to the maximum regulated amount. This will be rebated to customers in the following accounting year.

■ *Capital and reserves*—the increase of £58.9m is the amount of retained profit for the year as shown in the group profit and loss account, and reflects the increased total assets less liabilities attributable to shareholders.

OTHER ORGANIZATIONS

For non-limited companies the broad format and headings still apply but some items may be irrelevant and not appear, for example share capital, tax and dividends payable. An outline of the City of Newcastle upon Tyne's general fund balance sheet as at 31 March 1993[2] is shown in Figure 3.5.

CONSOLIDATED ACCOUNTS

A company can be a shareholder in another company. When a company owns more than 50 per cent of the voting capital in another company, the latter becomes a *subsidiary company* and the controlling company is called the *parent company*. This is commonplace in the UK and elsewhere. Each individual company must produce and distribute to its shareholders a set of annual accounts.

However, the various companies in a group are merely parts of one single undertaking and the parent company is obliged by law to present a consolidated set of accounts for the group's activities,

General fund balance sheet as at 31 March 1993

	£m
Net fixed assets	437.4
Investments	7.3
Debtors	6.1
Loans to other local authorities	20.7
Total long-term assets	471.5
Current assets	
Stocks and stores	2.4
Debtors	33.1
Investments	40.2
Cash balances	0.7
	76.4
Current liabilities	
Creditors	39.1
Borrowings and overdraft (short-term)	5.0
	44.1
Net current assets (76.4 - 44.1)	32.3
Provisions	12.5
Borrowings (long-term)	437.7
Deferred liabilities	20.1
Deferred credits	1.7
Total long-term liabilities	472.0
Total assets less liabilities (net assets) (471.5 + 76.4 − 44.1 − 472.0)	31.8
Total capital and revenue reserves	31.8

Figure 3.5 *Newcastle upon Tyne general fund balance sheet*

combining the separate accounts of the individual companies. The parent must prepare and send to its own shareholders:

■ a group profit and loss account;
■ a group balance sheet;
■ a group cash flow statement;
■ a parent company balance sheet.

In the case of the group balance sheet, some explanation is needed for some of the items that appear. The other statements are relatively straightforward and the explanations given for an individual company apply.

Consolidated balance sheet

There are a number of principles governing the combination of the separate balance sheets to obtain the consolidated balance sheet. Some of these principles are extremely complex and outside the scope of this book. The basic principles governing the consolidation of balance sheets include:

- fixed assets, current assets and external liabilities are amalgamated item by item;
- inter-company indebtedness is eliminated;
- the cost to the parent of the *investment in subsidiary companies* cancels out the shareholders' funds acquired in those subsidiaries;
- the amount of shareholders' funds in subsidiary companies that is owned by outside shareholders is shown separately as *minority interests*.

When a subsidiary is only partly owned, then all the assets (less debts) are not owned by the parent company even though they are shown in the consolidated balance sheet. Therefore, on consolidation, the value of these assets (less debts) owned by outsiders and referred to as minority interests is shown as a liability to arrive at the net assets owned by the parent company shareholders.

Example

A parent company (P Ltd) owns 80 per cent of a subsidiary (S 80% Ltd) which was set up in conjunction with another company which provided the other 20 per cent of the share capital.

The parent and subsidiary companies' balance sheets are set out below, in horizontal format for easy assimilation of the cross-references, together with the consolidated or group balance sheet.

P Ltd balance sheet

	£000		£000
Fixed assets	220	Issued share capital	300
Investment in S 80% Ltd	200*	Reserves	150
Loan to S 80% Ltd	50+		450
Current assets	30	Current liabilities	50
	500		500

S 80% Ltd balance sheet

	£000		£000
Fixed assets	350	Issued share capital	250 *
		Reserves	100
			350#

		Loan from P Ltd		50+
Current assets	<u>250</u>	Current liabilities		<u>200</u>
	<u>600</u>			<u>600</u>

P Ltd consolidated balance sheet

	£000				£000
Fixed assets	220		Issued share capital		300
	<u>350</u>	570	Reserves	150	
			(80% of S Ltd)	<u>80</u>	<u>230</u>
					530
			Minority interests		
			(20% x £350#)		70
Current assets	30		Current liabilities	50	
	<u>250</u>	<u>280</u>		<u>200</u>	<u>250</u>
		<u>850</u>			<u>850</u>

Note: The inter-company loan cross-referenced + cancels itself out. The investment in the subsidiary cross-referenced * cancels out 80 per cent of the issued share capital of the subsidiary. The other 20 per cent is part of minority interests cross-referenced #.

AUDIT

If you look at your own organization's annual report you will see a statement expressing an opinion that the financial statements give a true and fair view of the organization's affairs and comply with the relevant standards and legal requirements. Should this not be the case, the reader's attention would be drawn to the situation. Faced with such a threat, most organizations will go to some lengths to comply with all auditing requirements and obtain an unqualified report.

In large organizations, an internal audit function usually exists to check that systems and procedures are being carried out, and to help detect possible or actual fraud. This activity complements that of the external audit function.

Financial aspects of corporate governance

A committee chaired by Sir Adrian Cadbury made a number of recommendations to ensure best practice in the way that companies are managed at the top level.

Situations can arise where directors are perceived to be, even if they are not always actually, abusing their power. Companies are likely to be required in future to state that they comply with a code of best practice as laid down in the Cadbury Report. Some of the key requirements of the report include:

■ division of chairman and chief executive roles;
■ use of non-executive directors to bring independent judgement;
■ use of non-executive directors to set executives' remuneration package;
■ use of non-executive directors on audit committee;
■ interim reports to include a balance sheet reviewed by auditors;
■ disclosure of non-audit fees paid to auditors for other work.

SUMMARY

As with the profit and loss account or income statement, if you look at your own organization's balance sheet you will see two years' figures side by side. Again you can get a quick grasp of any significant changes by scanning the absolute values line by line.

Further insight might be gained by calculating the percentage changes from the previous year. The contents of Chapter 5 will give you greater insight into the balance sheet when we introduce accounting ratios and performance measures to monitor return on capital and the efficient use of assets. Further ratios measuring the riskiness of the capital structure and the solvency of the organization can also be calculated.

Changes are afoot to make the balance sheet more meaningful. The next year or two should see the debate clarifying its meaning and purpose. Other issues of topical interest relate to the valuation of assets; the inclusion of intangible assets, for example goodwill and brand values; and the disclosure of off-balance-sheet finance. An example of the latter is where a joint venture borrows capital which does not show in the consolidated balance sheet, hence disguising the true level of gearing. These topics are discussed in more detail in Chapter 6.

References

1. Northern Electric plc (1993) *Annual report and accounts.*
2. City of Newcastle upon Tyne (1992/3) *Annual report and accounts.*

4

Cash flow statement

When you look at the annual report and accounts of your own organization you will notice that there are three, not just two, financial statements. These are:

- an income statement (a profit and loss account or revenue account);
- a balance sheet;
- a cash flow statement.

A look at the first two statements will confirm that it is not easy to identify the cash flowing into and out of the business. For example, the profit and loss account includes transactions for which the cash settlement has not yet taken place, hence the need for debtors and creditors in the balance sheet. It also includes depreciation which is not a cash transaction as the cash was paid when the asset was originally purchased.

The balance sheet is a statement of assets and liabilities at a moment in time. It includes, however, some transactions that go back many years, for example fixed assets that were bought years ago or share capital that was subscribed when the the company was first formed.

A cash flow statement therefore summarizes exactly where cash came from and how it was spent. Because there is a time lag on many cash transactions, the statement is a mixture of items that refer to the current and the previous accounting year. Examples are tax and dividend payments that are partly paid in the year following the accounting year to which they relate. In fact, if payments in advance had been received from clients the statement could also include cash that related to the coming financial year.

For these reasons it is not possible to look at just this year's profit and loss account and balance sheet and produce a cash flow statement. We need the previous year's accounts and more than a little technical training! However, as a manager you need to know how to interpret a cash flow statement, not how to compile one.

WHAT IS IN THE STATEMENT?

Figure 4.1 gives an illustration of what the cash flow statement looks like in summary, omitting all the detailed items which would normally be included under each heading. Cash outflows are shown bracketed, cash inflows are not. Below we discuss exactly what is contained on each line.

	£000
Cash inflow from operating activities	1400
Returns on investment and servicing of finance	(350)
Tax paid	(400)
Investing activities	(870)
Net cash outflow before financing	(220)
Financing	300
Increase in cash and cash equivalents	80

Figure 4.1 *Outline of the cash flow statement*

Cash inflow from operating activities

Strictly speaking cash from operating activities need not be a net cash inflow, but could conceivably be an outflow, for example if the business incurs a loss which was not compensated by other items. This very important figure is a composite of a number of figures. They are detailed in an accompanying note to the statement to avoid adding too much detail to the statement itself. The individual items include:

- operating profit before interest and tax;
- depreciation added back (as it is not a cash expense);
- change in stock level from previous period-end;
- change in debtors level from previous period-end;
- change in creditors level from previous period-end.

The operating profit helps to generate cash, but not necessarily immediately due to credit transactions. This is allowed for by including changes in the debtors and creditors figures. Depreciation is charged against revenue as an expense and so reduces operating profit. However, as depreciation is not a cash transaction, any depreciation charged in the profit and loss account must be added back to operating profit to arrive at the underlying cash effect.

If the stock level has increased from the previous year-end, this is a use of cash. This is the case even if some of the stock has not yet been paid for, as such outstanding amounts will increase the creditors figure at this year-end. If the debtors figure has increased this means more credit has been granted to customers, using up more working capital. This is a cash outflow, but conversely a fall in debtors counts as a cash inflow. The change in creditors is the opposite to that in debtors: any increase in creditors is a source of cash, while a decrease in creditors uses up cash.

Returns on investment and servicing of finance

'Returns on investment and servicing of finance' is a relatively easy section of the statement to understand. It contains any interest and dividends received on investments made by the company, and any interest and dividends paid out. In most cases the net result will be an outflow of cash.

Tax paid

The tax referred to here is corporation tax, but it does not correspond exactly to the amount of tax shown in the profit and loss account for the same year. The tax actually paid out in an accounting year will relate partly to the previous year's profit and only partly to the current year's profit, because corporation tax is collected in instalments.

Investing activities

The investing activities section refers to the purchases and sales of fixed assets and investments in other businesses during the period. It represents the actual cash received or paid out.

Net cash flow before financing

'Net cash flow before financing' is the total of all the previous four sections, relating to the net cash inflow or outflow before any new finance is raised, or old finance repaid. It shows if the company is self-financing and therefore self-sufficient.

Financing

Both the issue and repayment of any loans, mortgages, debentures, finance leases or shares will show here. Borrowings from banks repayable within three months do not count as financing but are dealt with in the cash equivalents section later.

Changes in cash and cash equivalents

The final result of all the cash inflows and outflows above is reflected in the change in bank and cash balances at the end of the period. *Cash equivalents* are defined as short-term, highly liquid investments, capable of being converted into cash within a three-month maximum period.

Figure 4.2 shows a detailed cash flow statement including all the items discussed above. This uses what is described in FRS 1 as the *'indirect method'* when disclosing the *cash flow from operating activities*.

	£000	£000
Operating activities:		
Operating profit	1340	
Depreciation	280	
Increase in stocks	(170)	
Increase in debtors	(120)	
Increase in creditors	70	
Net cash inflow from operating activities		1400
Returns on investment and servicing of finance:		
Interest received	25	
Interest paid	(95)	
Dividends paid	(280)	
Net cash outflow from returns on investment and the servicing of finance		(350)
Tax paid		
UK Corporation tax	(395)	
Overseas tax	(5)	
Total tax paid		(400)
Investing activities:		
Purchase of tangible fixed assets	(990)	
Disposal of tangible fixed assets	120	
Net cash outflow on investing activities		(870)
Net cash outflow before financing		(220)
Financing activities:		
Repayment of loan	(150)	
Issue of ordinary share capital	450	
Net cash inflow from financing		300
Increase in cash and cash equivalents		80

Figure 4.2 *Detailed cash flow statement*

DIRECT AND INDIRECT METHODS

FRS 1,[1] dealing with the presentation of cash flow statements, became effective for accounting periods ending on 23 March 1992 onwards. It allows two alternative presentations of the net cash flow from operating activities, referred to as the direct method or the indirect method. The indirect method is more popular, perhaps because if the other method is chosen, a reconciliation with the first method is still required!

The direct method expresses the cash flow from operating profit in gross cash terms, not differentiating between current year's profit and working capital changes. The indirect method derives the cash flow from operating activities by taking the operating profit plus depreciation and the changes in working capital items. These figures are all easily traceable from the last profit and loss account and the last two balance sheets. Both approaches lead to the same net cash inflow from operating activities, as shown in Figure 4.3.

	£000
Direct method:	
Cash received from customers	9900
Cash payments to suppliers	(5200)
Cash paid to and on behalf of employees	(2700)
Other cash payments	(600)
Net cash inflow from operating activities	1400
Indirect method:	
Operating profit	1340
Depreciation	280
Increase in stocks	(170)
Increase in debtors	(120)
Increase in creditors	70
Net cash inflow from operating activities	1400

Figure 4.3 *Direct and indirect methods compared*

Interpretation of the statement

The statement in Figure 4.2 discloses that the company had a net cash outflow before financing of £220,000. An issue of £450,000 new share capital was undertaken, partly to finance this deficit and partly to repay an old loan of £150,000, leaving the remaining £80,000 to swell the cash and bank balances. Looking higher up the statement we now want to find reasons why the net cash outflow of £220,000 occurred.

The first calls on operating profit are net interest charges, taxation and dividends. Although these do not all relate exactly to the same time period they swallow up £750,000—over half of the £1,340,000 earned in the year. The remaining half of the operating profit plus the depreciation provision are available for new investment in working capital and fixed assets. It would appear to be the high level of investment in tangible fixed assets amounting to £990,000, well in excess of the depreciation provision of £280,000, that has resulted in the company not being totally self-financing and having to resort to new financing.

If the new investment in working capital and fixed assets reflects growth in the scale of operations, this new financing may be quite justified, providing an adequate return is earned on those new assets. This is a topic we return to in Chapter 10.

If, however, the new investment is merely the replacement of worn-out assets at today's new prices, the company may be guilty of not retaining sufficient cash to allow for their replacement at current prices. The level of dividend payment shown as £280,000 does not seem high relative to operating profit after tax payments, so this possibility seems unlikely.

Having discussed the layout and interpretation of cash flow statements at some length, we can now examine the published group cash flow statement for Northern Electric plc[2] shown in Figure 4.4. This is of course compatible with Northern Electric's group profit and loss account and group balance sheet previously illustrated.

Group statement of cash flows for the year ended 31 March

	1993 £m	1992 £m
Net cash flow from operating activities	151.7	121.4
Returns on investment and servicing of finance		
Interest received	3.4	0.9
Interest paid	(9.1)	(10.2)
Dividends received	8.0	7.0
Dividends paid	(23.8)	(20.8)
Net cash outflow from returns on investments and the servicing of finance	(21.5)	(23.1)
Taxation		
Corporation tax paid (including ACT on dividends)	(23.6)	(23.7)

	1993 £m	1992 £m
Investing activities		
Payments to acquire tangible fixed assets	(67.7)	(59.8)
Receipts from sales of tangible fixed assets	2.0	0.6
Receipt of consumers' contributions	13.9	15.0
Payments to acquire investments	(34.6)	(2.7)
Net cash outflow from investing activities	(86.4)	(46.9)
Net cash inflow before financing	20.2	27.7
Financing		
Issue of ordinary share capital	(0.1)	-
Repayment of amounts borrowed	-	90.0
Net cash outflow/(inflow) from financing	(0.1)	90.0
Increase/(decrease) in cash and cash equivalents	20.3	(62.3)
	20.2	27.7

Note: The standard FRS 1 reverses the bracket convention for a group of companies in the financing section of the statement.

Figure 4.4 *Published cash flow statement for Northern Electric plc*

The statement shows that the Northern Electric Group was self-sufficient for cash in the year ended March 1993, generating sufficient funds not just to make tax and dividend payments, but also to finance relatively large acquisitions of tangible fixed assets (£67.7m) and long-term investments (£34.6m). After all these payments, the group still managed to increase its cash and cash equivalents by £20m.

Contained in a note to the accounts is an explanation of the make-up of the net cash flow from operating activities, shown as £151.7m at the top of the statement for 1993. This reveals:

	£m
Operating profit	106.4
Depreciation charges	19.7
Increase in provisions	17.4
Decrease in stocks	1.1
Increase in debtors	(3.7)
Increase in creditors	10.8
	151.7

The increase in provisions of £17.4m was the net amount charged in the 1993 profit and loss account for liabilities and charges relating to the year but which will be settled in cash later. A large part of this £17.4m relates to an overrecovery of electricity supply and distribution revenue compared to the maximum regulated amounts set by Offer, the regulatory body. Even if the provisions made in 1993 had all been spent in the same year the group would have still been cash positive, as the increased cash and cash equivalent balances of £20.3m exceeded this £17.4m provision.

In the previous year Northern Electric Group was also self-sufficient for cash before financing, generating some £27.7m in all. The repayment of a loan of £90m to the government resulted in the large decrease in cash and cash equivalents of £62.3m built up over previous years.

SUMMARY

In this chapter we have examined the third and final financial statement making up the trio that we call the financial accounts. Although this cash flow statement is used primarily by senior management and financial advisers, it is important that all managers are aware of its broad content and meaning. Never has so much attention been paid to cash flow as during the recession at the end of the 1980s and early 1990s.

You should now be able to recognize how cash is generated by trading profitably and how it can be absorbed on working capital and expenditure on fixed assets. Whatever management role you have, at whatever level, it is likely that you play a part in either the generation or the spending of that cash. Decisions that you make, or policies that you have to follow, will be partly influenced by the cash position in your organization.

At the time of writing, FRS 1 has been in operation for two years and is the subject of a review by the Accounting Standards Board. The Board will be looking, in particular, at the definition of cash and cash equivalents. This classifies deposits over three months as investments and not as a cash equivalent and has been the subject of criticism by leading finance directors.

References

1. Accounting Standards Board (1991) FRS 1: *Cash flow statements*, London.
2. Northern Electric plc (1993) *Annual report and accounts*, Newcastle upon Tyne.

5

Accounting ratios

P revious chapters have introduced financial statements without saying too much about their interpretation. There are a number of ways that performance can be measured from these statements, and further insights can be gained into aspects of a company's financial performance regarding profitability, efficiency, liquidity, capital structure and investment potential. We can:

- examine the absolute change in amount from the previous year item by item;
- calculate the relative change from the previous year for each item as a percentage;
- compare the latest year's figures with budgeted figures for the same period;
- use an analytical approach by relating pairs of figures together as *accounting ratios.*

An experienced person can gain some insight into a company's affairs by an examination of absolute and percentage changes in figures. You may have heard reporting in the media that a certain company made £x million profit last year, or an increase of £y million profit over the

Example

A company increased its profit by 10 per cent over the previous year. Taken in isolation this may appear to be a good performance. However, if the fixed assets and the working capital (the capital employed) had increased by 20 per cent in the same period, this is not so good because the percentage *return on capital employed* will have fallen. In other words, the absolute value of profit is not as meaningful as its relative value, expressed as either the return on capital employed or the profit margin on sales.

previous year. If this was a brewery, and a further announcement was made that it was increasing prices by 5p per pint, your likely reaction is understandable! Such statements can sometimes be misleading.

A more methodical and analytical approach is needed to supplement the broadbrush look at changes from year to year. In a profit-seeking company this requires the identification of related pairs of figures taken from the profit and loss and/or balance sheet. These relationships are called *ratios* even though many are expressed as percentages or functions.

For example, when profit is £1m and capital employed is £5m this is normally expressed as a return on capital of 20 per cent. This could equally well be described as a 1:5 profit to capital ratio, or that capital was five times the profit figure. Convention largely dictates the form in which a ratio is expressed.

Some ratios are meaningful as an absolute value, but they are mainly used in a comparative way, with for example:

■ the same ratio in the previous year;
■ a target ratio;
■ a competitor's ratio.

We now examine the ratios used to measure aspects of a company's financial performance.

PROFITABILITY RATIOS

There are three key ratios that hold the clue to company profitability. These are:

■ *return on capital employed*—the real test if profit is adequate or not is profit expressed as a percentage of the capital employed in financing the assets used by the business. This depends on the next two ratios;
■ *profit margin*—net and/or gross profit expressed as a percentage of sales;
■ *turnover of capital employed*—how many £ of sales have been generated with each £1 of capital employed. As the capital is used to finance the assets, this ratio really measures the intensity of use of fixed assets and the control of working capital items such as debtors and stocks.

Note that some companies actually substitute net assets plus long-term creditors for capital employed and calculate operating profit as a percentage of this figure. However, capital employed and net assets plus long-term creditors are two faces of the same coin with the same value.

Example

When operating profit is £1m, sales are £10m and capital employed is £5m, the following ratios emerge:

$$\frac{\text{Profit } £1m}{\text{Capital } £5m} = 20\% \qquad \frac{\text{Profit } £1m}{\text{Sales } £10m} = 10\% \qquad \frac{\text{Sales } £10m}{\text{Capital } £5m} = 2 \text{ times}$$

Return on capital 20% = Profit margin 10% × Rate of turnover of capital 2 times

The return on capital varies from one industry to another and even from firm to firm within the same industry. Capital-intensive industries, like electricity generation and supply, typically have high profit margins to compensate for a low rate of turnover of capital. In the 1992/3 annual accounts for Scottish Hydro-Electric plc, for example, operating profit was 24.6 per cent of turnover but the turnover of capital was only 0.8 times based on historical cost accounting.

In contrast, the Balfour Beatty civil engineering group, operating in a labour- and material-intensive industry which hires a lot of plant and equipment, had an operating profit to turnover ratio of 2.1 per cent for the calendar year 1992 and a turnover of capital of about 11 times.

The above three key ratios are only a starting point. Further analysis of the profit and loss account and balance sheet can help to identify where management action is needed to improve financial performance, as the diagram in Figure 5.1 shows.

The following discussion relates to the precise definition and meaning of each ratio, putting them in the context in which they are used. Actual figures are drawn from the Northern Electric plc annual report and accounts for the year ended 31 March 1993.

Most of the figures used can be found in Northern Electric's group profit and loss account and group balance sheet, illustrated in Chapters 2 and 3 respectively. Other figures are extracted from the notes to the accounts contained in that report[1].

Return on capital

Both profit and capital are capable of a number of interpretations, so it is important to know the precise definition being used by a particular company. If we want to examine profitability, then a suitable pairing is the profit on ordinary activities before interest and tax as a percentage of the total capital employed. This gives us a view of the overall profitability of the company irrespective of whose capital has been used

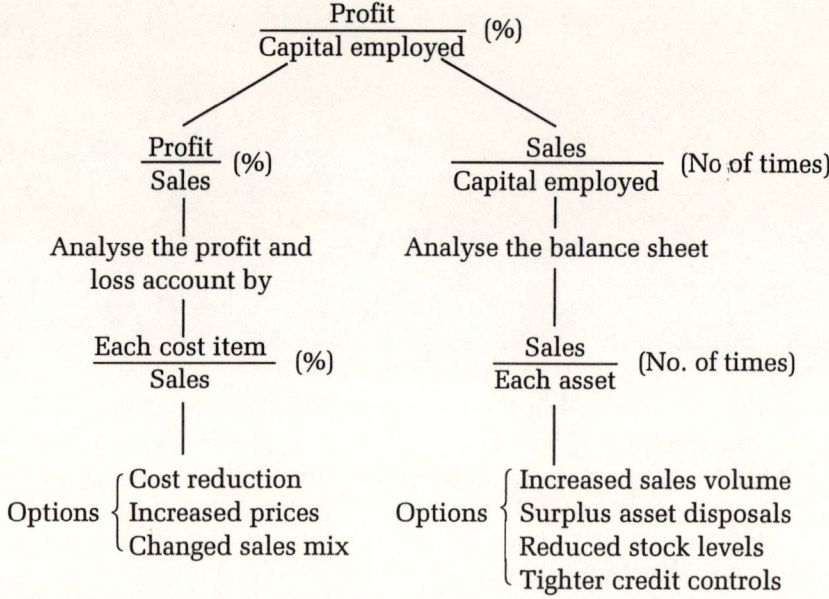

$$\frac{\text{Profit}}{\text{Capital employed}} \text{ (\%)}$$

$$\frac{\text{Profit}}{\text{Sales}} \text{ (\%)} \qquad\qquad \frac{\text{Sales}}{\text{Capital employed}} \text{ (No of times)}$$

Analyse the profit and   Analyse the balance sheet
loss account by

$$\frac{\text{Each cost item}}{\text{Sales}} \text{ (\%)} \qquad\qquad \frac{\text{Sales}}{\text{Each asset}} \text{ (No. of times)}$$

Options $\begin{cases} \text{Cost reduction} \\ \text{Increased prices} \\ \text{Changed sales mix} \end{cases}$ Options $\begin{cases} \text{Increased sales volume} \\ \text{Surplus asset disposals} \\ \text{Reduced stock levels} \\ \text{Tighter credit controls} \end{cases}$

Monitoring these ratios over time and measuring actual performance against targets, benchmarking and interfirm comparisons (see later) can lead to any of the above actions by management to improve financial performance.

Figure 5.1 *Ratios leading to management action*

and ignores the tax shield on interest payments explained in Chapter 10. For Northern Electric plc, income from investments (£10.7m) is added to operating profit (£106.4m) to give £117.1m as the profit on ordinary activities before interest and tax.

One basic definition of capital employed is *'total assets less current liabilities'*, which is what the capital actually finances. It is sometimes a source of confusion that accountants can describe capital employed either in terms of the assets on which the finance was spent, or in terms of the various sources of finance. The value of capital employed is specifically disclosed in all balance sheets as total assets less current liabilities.

Some companies reduce this total amount by the value of cash and bank balances to find the net capital employed. Other companies include creditors for tax and dividends owing as part of capital employed, on the grounds that the company usually has use of these funds for many months before they are paid out. Another possible adjustment is to average out the capital employed at the beginning and end of the year to get a more representative figure than is given by using the latest year-end only. Northern Electric plc carry out all of these fine-tunings. The make-up of their average capital employed of £488.4m for the year 1992/3 is shown in Figure 5.2.

	1993	1992	
Group capital employed	*£m*	*£m*	
Shareholders' funds	424.7	365.7	
Loan capital	74.0	74.0	
Dividends payable	18.6	16.0	
Corporation tax and ACT payable	27.0	26.6	
Cash and investments	(35.1)	(14.8)	
	509.2	467.5	(Average £488.4m)

Figure 5.2 *Northern Electric plc average capital employed*

Using the above definitions of profit and capital employed gives a 24.0 per cent return on capital, based on historical cost accounting.

The audited accounts of Northern Electric plc include a set of financial statements prepared under the current cost accounting convention. This topic is explained in Chapter 6 in relation to British Gas plc, but essentially the convention allows for price changes specific to the business when reporting assets employed and profits earned.

A utility like Northern Electric plc has very long-life assets. If these assets are valued at their current cost, and depreciation calculated on this basis, the return on average capital employed is 9.1 per cent compared with 24.0 per cent on an historical cost basis. Business decisions need to be based on current cost accounting information in this type of industry.

Return on shareholders' funds

A narrower view of return on capital, looking at it just from a shareholder's viewpoint, takes the profit after tax attributable to members of the parent company (£85.3m) and expresses it as a percentage of the average shareholders' funds (£395.2m), being the sum of share capital and reserves invested in the business by shareholders. The resulting return on shareholders' funds is 21.6 per cent on a historical cost accounting basis.

Profit margins

The profitability of sales can be measured in most industries at two levels by the gross and net margins. The gross margin is calculated by expressing the gross profit (£271.6m) as a percentage of sales turnover (£882.7m) to give 30.8 per cent. This helps monitor both the cost of sales and selling prices. The net margin of 12.0 per cent is based on the operating profit (£106.4m) as a percentage of sales turnover (£882.7m), thus taking account of the overheads ignored in the gross margin. The use of both gross and net margins helps to identify the level where any improvement or problem has arisen.

Note that the operating profit is used in preference to the profit on ordinary activities before interest, as a more compatible figure with the turnover. This is because the income from investments is not related to the sales turnover figure and differs in this respect from our choice of the profit figure to relate to capital employed.

Turnover of capital

If we divide the sales turnover (£882.7m) for the year by the average capital employed (£488.4m) we find out that £1.81 of sales have been generated in 1992/3 by each £1 of capital employed. An alternative way of putting this is to say that capital has been turned over 1.81 times in the year. The result says much about the efficiency with which the assets have been managed and the use of creditors to help finance the business. This can be further analysed by the following asset utilization ratios.

ASSET UTILIZATION RATIOS

There are four ratios to determine the efficiency with which assets are managed. These are:

■ sales/fixed assets;
■ sales/working capital;
■ sales/stocks;
■ sales/debtors.

Sales/fixed assets

When tangible fixed assets of £361.5m are divided into the sales turnover (£882.7m) for the year it tells how intensively each £1 of hardware has been used to generate sales within the year. The answer in this case is 2.44 times, and it is a case of the greater the better.

Sales/working capital

Working capital is defined as current assets less current liabilities in balance sheet terms, but it can be thought of as money continuously circulating round the company. An old-fashioned term for working capital is 'circulating capital', which is more descriptive in some ways. Money is first needed to pay for employees' work effort. Then it is needed to pay for materials and overheads which are eventually recovered when the customer pays up. In most industries the company providing goods and services is always out of pocket, with more money outstanding from customers and tied up in stocks than it owes to its own suppliers. The faster that working capital is turned over, the more sales are generated from each £1 of working capital, so again, the bigger this ratio the better.

In Northern Electric's case, sales turnover of £882.7m divided by working capital of £82.0m shows that each £1 of working capital was turned over 10.8 times. This very healthy ratio is greatly influenced by the fact that the basic product of electricity cannot be stored, thus obviating the need for stocks and work in progress relating to electricity supply; this is not of course true regarding the company's retail and contracting activities.

Some industries even manage to work on negative working capital, whereby they owe more money to short-term creditors than the value of their current assets. A case in point is the contracting and civil engineering industries, where advance payments and monthly progress payments keep down the work in progress to very modest amounts relative to the value of the contracts being worked on. The 1992 Balfour Beatty Group annual report and accounts reveals working capital of £100.1m and turnover of £1.881bn, giving a multiple of 18.8 times.

Sales/stocks

The sales/stocks ratio is a crude guide to stock turnover. A better measure is obtained from cost of sales/stocks so that both are measured in cost price rather than one at cost price and the other at selling price.

IT systems used by larger organizations will provide this kind of data in detail, for each operating unit. A more general global picture can be derived from the annual accounts by dividing turnover by stocks.

Dividing Northern Electric's turnover of £882.7m by £9.5m stocks gives the astronomical figure of 92.9 times for the stock turnover rate. This reinforces the point made earlier that the bulk of the sales turnover relates to energy sales but electricity itself cannot be stored.

Sales/debtors

For the sales/debtors ratio the annual sales are divided by the year-end debtors figure to tell us how many times a year the debtors are paying up on average. If the answer is, say, six times, then debtors are taking two months to pay. By inverting the ratio and multiplying by 365 days we can get the answer as so many days, for example:

$$\text{Credit period taken by customers} = \frac{\text{Debtors}}{\text{Sales}} \times 365 = \frac{£169.3m}{£882.7m} \times 365 = 70 \text{days}$$

Here again, IT systems can provide much more detail on debtor age analysis by giving an overall picture and breaking total debtors down into categories by lengths of time. This may be vital as credit control needs to be exercised throughout the year and not just at the year-end. A snapshot view may also not be typical of the experience during the rest of the year, particularly if there are seasonal peaks and troughs and different businesses involved.

Sales/creditors

Sales/creditors is obviously not an asset utilization ratio! If, however, creditors are used to finance assets, then the more credit taken and the longer the time to pay suppliers, the less working capital will be needed by the buying company. Although the sales/creditors ratio will give a crude guide, the purchases/creditors ratio is more accurate and IT systems again will provide an abundance of data. The figure of total purchases is not disclosed in published annual accounts.

We now look at a different aspect of a company's performance—the extent to which it is financed by borrowings and if they are excessive—then turning to measures of solvency and the use of accounting ratios to help predict corporate failure.

GEARING AND SOLVENCY RATIOS

During the UK recession of 1989—1993, much was heard and talked of gearing ratios. Many companies went into liquidation during this period and high gearing was a common cause, particularly in the case of construction companies. More generally, a lack of cash led many companies into receivership through their inability to generate enough cash to pay trade creditors, repay bankers, or settle their tax bills.

Gearing

Gearing is the relationship of borrowings to shareholders' funds. A company is said to be highly geared when its borrowings are a high proportion of the equity, usually expressed as a percentage (see Figure 5.3). Conversely, low gearing applies when borrowings are a small percentage of shareholders' funds.

	High gearing	*Low gearing*
Borrowings	50%	10%
Shareholders' funds	50%	90%
Total capital	100%	100%

Figure 5.3 *Example of high and low gearing*

Northern Electric plc had a low gearing level of 9.2 per cent as at 31 March 1993. Borrowings, after cash and short-term investments were netted off, amounted to £38.9m compared with £424.7m of shareholders' funds.

There are two risks involved with high gearing. One is the capital risk that loans cannot be repaid when due. Either more profits have to be retained to repay loans when they mature, or new loans need to be taken out, or a rights issue of shares has to be made. In normal times any of these may be possible but at times of severe recession, if losses rather than profits are being made, then none of the options to repay loans is really feasible. The second risk relates to the interest payments, that insufficient profit is generated from trading activities with which to pay them.

Interest cover

The interest cover measures the degree of security relating to the interest payments. The more times the profit covers the interest payments, the less risk to the lenders and to the other providers of capital. Shareholders' dividends come last in the queue: if a high proportion of profits is used up in interest payments, little remains for the owners of the business.

Interest cover is the number of times that profit before interest covers the annual interest payments. In Northern Electric's case, its net interest payments of £5.7m are covered a massive 20.5 times by the profit of £117.1m. Alternatively, as the company itself puts it, net interest payments amount to 4.9 per cent of the profit before interest. This should pose little risk to any party.

Bankers often set covenants on interest cover and gearing levels, which, if breached, lead to a renegotiation of the loans with a possible request for their repayment immediately.

Why then do companies bother with gearing at all? We saw in Chapter 3 that all interest payments attract tax relief, while dividends do not. Also we mentioned that if a company can earn more profit by using borrowed capital in its business, in excess of the cost of the interest payments, the surplus profits belong to the shareholders and enhance their earnings per share.

Therefore, it is probably fair to say that a little gearing is a good thing, but too much gearing can damage a company's health. This makes it sound like all the other vices!

LIQUIDITY RATIOS

There are two somewhat similar tests of a company's ability to pay its way and settle its short-term debts. These are the *current ratio* and the *acid test ratio*. The current ratio divides all current assets (£213.9m) by current liabilities (£131.9m, creditors due within a year), giving a ratio of 1.62:1 for Northern Electric plc. As debtors and cash and short-term investments well exceed short-term creditors, there is no liquidity problem evident here.

There is no norm figure we can quote that is universally applicable to any firm in any industry. Just-in-time techniques, invoice factoring and prepayments by clients are just a few examples of what would cause the current ratio to vary between firms, even in the same industry.

Individual industries have their own peculiarities regarding the existence of certain types of stocks or work in progress, and contractual arrangements between debtors and creditors vary widely. Better by far to examine the trend over time for the same company to get a feel for what is happening.

The *acid test ratio* is calculated in the same way as the current ratio, except that stocks and work in progress are omitted from current assets on the grounds of illiquidity. This makes little difference in the case of Northern Electric plc, reducing the 1.62:1 current ratio to 1.55:1 on an acid test basis, still more than adequate.

In theory it might seem that only a 1:1 ratio is needed, but the terms of sale for both debtors and creditors may need close scrutiny. The contracting industry might manage on less than a 1:1 ratio if money is received from clients before many of its creditors are paid. With long time intervals before proposed dividends and corporation tax payments need to be made, a careful analysis of all short-term creditors is needed before conclusions can be drawn. In any event, a cash flow forecast is an essential tool if short- and long-term commitments are to be managed effectively.

PREDICTING BUSINESS FAILURE

Some researchers have suggested that a combination of a number of ratios can be used to assess the financial health of a company and its likely success or failure. Various combinations of ratios, and various weightings of them, have been tried by different researchers to give a single measure, known as a 'Z score'. Altman was first in the field and he combined the following five ratios (weightings in brackets) as a result of his research into 66 manufacturing companies in the US:[2]

1. Net current assets/total assets (1.2)—defines the asset structure.
2. Retained earnings/total assets (1.4)—puts retentions in context of the company size.
3. Profit (pre interest and tax)/total assets (3.3)—a measure of return on capital.
4. Market value of equity/book value of debt (0.6)—a type of gearing ratio.
5. Sales/total assets (1.0)—a measure of turnover of capital.

To illustrate this approach, assumed values have been taken for each ratio which is then multiplied by its own weight, and the final Z score calculated:

	Assumed value of ratio	Weight	Weighted value
1. Net current assets/total assets	0.50	1.2	0.60
2. Retained earnings/total assets	0.60	1.4	0.84
3. Profit (pre interest and tax)/total assets	0.15	3.3	0.50
4. Market value of equity/book value of debt	2.00	0.6	1.20
5. Sales/total assets	2.00	1.0	2.00
		Z score	5.14

Altman found that companies with Z scores of above 3.0 were unlikely to fail, while scores below 1.8 gave cause for concern about failure in the coming year or two. You can see that the company in the above example would be quite safe on this measure.

Some words of caution are appropriate. This research was conducted some years ago and the sample was restricted to manufacturing companies in America, so its use elsewhere, and in different industries, was not intended. Since then, changes in work practices, with regard to just-in-time for stocks and the growing practice of financing debtors by factoring, would require Altman's model to be amended even for US manufacturing companies.

If you have an interest in models to predict corporate failure in the UK or elsewhere, you will find the résumé by Smith[3] of interest. His article comments on a number of other articles on this topic in recent years.

VALUE ADDED

The idea of value added has widespread use in measuring employee performance and for relating pay incentives to the value added in a period of time. A broad definition of value added is:

Value added = Sales less bought-in goods and services

The wealth created by any business is the value of its sales less the cost of all bought-in goods and services, which are the wealth created by other organizations. All firms are creators of wealth. They buy in raw materials and services and use labour and equipment to convert or process these resources into products and services, which in turn they sell to their own customers. The difference between the final sales value and the original bought-in cost of materials and services is the value added by the firm.

The calculation of value added uses the same information as a profit and loss account, but sets it out with a different perspective. The profit and loss account is directed at the shareholders of the company. The value added statement is neutral and focuses on the total wealth created for all the four interested parties, namely:

- employees;
- government;
- providers of capital;
- company.

You may find it useful to compare a profit and loss account with a value added statement prepared from exactly the same data, illustrated in Figure 5.4.

Profit and loss account

		£000	£000
Sales 1000			
Less:	Materials used*	300	
	Services purchased*	130	
	Wages and salaries	350	
	Depreciation+	90	
	Interest on loan	50	920
Profit before tax			80
Corporation tax on profit			30
Profit after tax			50
Dividends			30
Retained profit+			20

Value added statement

	£000
Sales	1000
Less: Bought-in materials and services (300 and 130 marked * above)	430
Value added	570

The value added was distributed:

To employees—as wages, salaries, employer's pension and NI contributions.	350
To government—as corporation tax on profit	30
To providers of capital—as interest and dividends	80
To reinvestment—depreciation plus retained profit (90 and 20 marked + above)	110
	570

Figure 5.4 *Profit and loss account and value added statements compared*

It can be argued that in some firms the proportion of wealth going to one or two parties has been too large, resulting in too small a distribution elsewhere. A classic trade-off is between labour and/or dividends as opposed to capital reinvestment. Too much cash going out of the business leaves too little for reinvestment, and is possibly a cause of some declining industries.

Some financial experts have commented that, in many of the UK's declining industries, the level of reinvestment has been too low to keep the country competitive internationally. Others have pointed to poor productivity which results in low value added, low reinvestment, and an apparently high distribution of wealth to labour. This debate lies at the heart of how the UK is to improve its economic performance as a nation, particularly on the manufacturing front. Some improvement in productivity and reinvestment levels was evident in the 1980s, sometimes aided by Japanese capital and changes to methods of manufacturing.

Value added ratios

Labour productivity can be measured and monitored in broad terms using the concept of value added. Two value added ratios are appropriate:

$$Value\ added\ per\ employee = \frac{total\ value\ added}{number\ of\ employees}$$

$$Wages\ and\ salaries\ per\ £1\ of\ value\ added = \frac{total\ wages\ and\ salaries\ bill}{total\ value\ added}$$

Consideration should be given to whether to base the value added statement on a historical cost or current cost basis. The latter would seem more appropriate because only then can we talk about the real value of wealth created by a company. Current cost accounting is explained in Chapter 6.

PUBLIC SECTOR

Most of the ratios and discussion so far in this chapter has had little relevance for public sector organizations which are not profit oriented, and do not have owners seeking a return on capital in most cases. The government, however, does set a return on capital objective for some activities under its control.

Ratios that have a role to play in measuring the performance of public sector services are often referred to as the 3 Es:

■ economy;
■ efficiency;
■ effectiveness.

These relate to various measurements of inputs and outputs and play an important role in the auditing of public sector activities and the quest for *value for money*.

Yardsticks can be used for monitoring service activities in both public and private sector. This can take the the form of relating the cost of carrying out a certain activity to the output achieved, so deriving a cost per unit. Benchmarking, mentioned later, is as applicable to public sector organizations as to those in the private sector.

Examples drawn from various service activities could be:

■ Local authority—the cost of refuse disposal per household.
■ Hospital—the cost per patient bed/day.
■ Bank—the cost per cheque clearance.
■ Haulage contractor—running costs per tonne/mile.
■ Electricity company—cost per meter reading.

INTERORGANIZATION COMPARISONS

It is possible to make comparisons of one organization with another in a number of ways:

■ self-analysis using data drawn from other organizations' annual reports;
■ credit agency reports;
■ using the Centre for Interfirm Comparisons;
■ trade associations' data;
■ government reports.

You can usually obtain a copy of the annual report and accounts from most organizations on request. In the case of a limited company, most of the accounting ratios mentioned here can be calculated from the information provided, if not already in the annual report as part of a summary of financial data for the last few years.

Alternatively, use can be made of a credit agency like Dun and Bradstreet which compiles ratios and other statistics to help clients form a view on the creditworthiness of existing and potential clients. Your organization may have used such a service or provided this kind of data.

Trade associations often compile data on the financial performance of their members and produce norm ratios. The Centre for Interfirm Comparisons conducts studies for particular industries and produces ratios for the participating companies anonymously. A participant can therefore scrutinize the ratios of competitors and compare itself to the average within a best/worst range. The Central Statistical Office is also a source of much information on public sector activities and performance.

A useful article by Wilson[4] examines the techniques available in the area of competitor analysis as a background to developing a strategy towards an enhanced competitive position.

On a wider front, CIMA has published a number of research findings on measuring business performance in both manufacturing and service sectors; see the Bibliography.

Benchmarking

The term benchmarking is used to describe an extension of the interorganization comparison approach which is limited to a comparison with competitors, mainly restricted to financial measurements.

Benchmarking is an ongoing process to improve products, services and systems by reference to the best practices that can be found anywhere. It focuses on the key operational processes within a business that are critical to its success or failure. Best practice organizations are studied to discover any differences in practices and processes that could be transferred. An article by Hazell and Morrow linking performance measurement and benchmarking is helpful here.[5]

INVESTMENT RATIOS

Returning now to private sector companies, with the emphasis on those quoted on the Stock Exchange, there are a number of other ratios used by investors, potential investors and financial advisers to assess financial performance from an investment viewpoint. You will probably have seen and read about these financial ratios in the press. The main ones include:

- market capitalization;
- earnings per share;
- price/earnings ratio;
- dividend yield;
- dividend cover.

Again we will draw on Northern Electric plc and information contained in its annual report and accounts for the year ended 31 March 1993. The market price of its shares on 24 March 1994 was 654p.

Market capitalization

Market capitalization denotes the size of a company in terms of its total market value. There are 123m shares issued by Northern Electric plc, so on 24 March 1994 its market capitalization was £805m. This information is useful to investors because the larger the company, the easier it is to buy or sell large quantities of shares. It is also cheaper because the spread, or difference between the buying and selling prices of a share, becomes proportionately smaller as the market capitalization increases.

Earnings per share

You may recall earnings per share (eps) from Chapter 2 as the bottom line on a profit and loss account—quite literally. It is calculated from the profit earned for ordinary shareholders after tax, divided by the number of ordinary shares in issue.

$$eps = \frac{profit\ after\ tax}{no.\ of\ ordinary\ shares\ issued} = \frac{£85.3m}{123m} = 69.3p$$

Performance is monitored by comparing the eps from year to year for the same company, although FRS 3 attempted to break this long-standing habit. We return to this theme in Chapter 6.

Price/earnings ratio

We can not compare the *earnings per share* from one company to another because the size of companies and the number of shares issued vary widely. The *price/earnings ratio* (p/e) is a means of comparing the stock market's assessment of a listed company's shares. It is found by dividing the latest market price of a share by its latest annual earnings per share. In the case of Northern Electric plc, 654p divided by 69.3p gives a p/e ratio of 9.4 on 24 March 1994. This was at the lower end of the p/e ratios for regional electricity companies which at that time were in the range 9.4–12.5.

Companies with low p/e ratios are not expected to increase profits and/or dividends as fast as those with high p/e multiples. Lower p/e ratios may also suggest a higher element of risk than higher ones. The average p/e ratio in the UK is traditionally found in the teens, but has been in the low twenties of late in the expectation of a strong recovery in corporate earnings as the country climbs out of recession.

Dividend yield

Not all of the earnings per share are paid out as dividends. The dividend yield ratio looks at the income received by an investor as a percentage of the present market price. The dividend is shown gross of income tax so that the yield can be compared with that on other investments, irrespective of the tax position of an individual investor. Northern Electric's gross dividend was 26.81p per share with a market price of 654p:

$$\text{Dividend yield} = \frac{26.81p}{654p} \% = 4.1\%$$

Ignoring expenses, any investor buying Northern Electric plc shares on 24 March 1994 would get a gross income of 4.1 per cent if the previous year's dividend was repeated. This raises an important point of difference between newspapers' treatment of interim figures. Some newspapers base eps, p/e ratio and dividend yield on the last 12 months' reported figures, combining two half-years if appropriate. Other papers use the approach we have adopted and base the ratios on the last full year reported by the company.

Dividend cover

The final ratio looks at the dividend from a security angle, asking the question of how many times the earnings per share covers the dividend per share—once more a case of the bigger the better. This is very much akin to the interest cover ratio mentioned earlier. With an earnings per share of 69.3p and a net dividend actually paid by the company of 21.45p (80 per cent of the gross dividend), then for Northern Electric plc:

$$\text{Dividend cover} = \frac{69.3p}{21.45p} = 3.2 \text{ times}$$

The proportion of profit paid out as dividend varies from one company to another depending on the perceived needs of the company's investors as well as its need to retain profits for expansion. Once a dividend policy has been established it must be adhered to, and dividends thereafter follow the trend of profits over the years.

Any sudden drop in the dividend usually has an adverse effect on the share price of the company concerned. This is avoided whenever possible, even when the dividend payout is not covered by earnings, if a quick recovery in profits is expected.

SUMMARY

The ratios we have discussed are not just ways of measuring financial performance in the past. They also have an invaluable role to play in setting financial objectives, or as targets to aim for in the future.

Some of the ratios are only applicable to profit-seeking companies. Other ratios and yardsticks that give some measure of *cost per unit*, irrespective of whether that is a product or a service activity, are of value to any organization.

We pick up these themes again in later chapters on costing and budgeting. Meanwhile, if you want a wider view of the use of management ratios related to functional activities of a business, try reading Westwick's book, listed in the Bibliography.

Obtain a set of annual accounts for your own organization and calculate appropriate ratios from the two years' data given. Try to form a view on whether the financial performance has got better or worse during this period. Alternatively, use the accounts for Northern Electric plc already provided in Chapters 2 and 3 and calculate the previous year's ratios, so far as you can, to compare with those given in this chapter.

References

1. Northern Electric plc (1993) Annual report and accounts.
2. Altman, E I (1968) 'Financial ratios, discriminant analysis and the prediction of corporate bankruptcy', *Journal of Finance* (USA), September.
3. Smith, M (1992) 'Corporate failure prediction: some misconceptions corrected', *Management Accounting* (UK), December.
4. Wilson, R M S (1994) 'Competitor analysis', *Management Accounting* (UK), April.
5. Hazell, M and Morrow, M (1992) 'Performance measurement and benchmarking', *Management Accounting* (UK), December.

6

Issues in financial reporting

This chapter discusses a number of topics on financial reporting, which were flagged up in previous chapters as needing further explanation. Some of these are contentious issues among accountants and/or between practitioners and the Accounting Standards Board.

We shall examine:

■ FRS 3—reporting financial performance;
■ the definition of earnings per share;
■ current cost accounting;
■ the valuation of intangible assets.

REPORTING FINANCIAL PERFORMANCE

The Financial Reporting Standard FRS 3, entitled *Reporting Financial Performance*, was effective for accounting periods ending on 22 June 1993 and thereafter. This standard aims to make the profit and loss account more informative and less open to creative accounting via the use of exceptional and extraordinary items. It is also intended to contain sufficient information so that a sole concentration on earnings per share can be avoided.

FRS 3 requires companies to:

■ separate sales or turnover and operating profit between continuing operations, acquisitions and discontinued operations;
■ disclose profits and losses resulting from restructuring/reorganization or from the disposal of fixed assets or parts of the business;

- disclose extraordinary items (which should now be a rare event!) and exceptional items, and to calculate earnings per share after taking them into account;
- prepare a statement of total recognized gains and losses in the period to embrace the profit for the year and other gains or losses arising, for example from any revaluation of assets or the effect of currency movements on overseas asset values;
- prepare a reconciliation of movements in shareholders' funds between the start and end of the period including retained profit; other recognized gains or losses; goodwill written off or back from reserves; and new share capital subscribed.

An example of the new format is shown in Figure 6.1 in respect of John Menzies plc group profit and loss account[1] for the year ending 1 May 1993, complying with FRS 3 although not mandatory at the time. Also included are the statement of total recognized gains and losses, and the reconciliation of movements in shareholders' funds.

Group profit and loss account

	1993		1992 restated	
	£m	£m	£m	£m
Turnover				
Continuing operations		1143.8		1061.7
Discontinued operations		24.3		38.8
		1168.1		1100.5
Net operating costs		1136.6		1071.0
Operating profit				
Continuing operations	32.0		29.8	
Discontinued operations	(0.5)	31.5	(0.3)	29.5
Discontinued US operation:				
Provision set up	—		(3.1)	
Cost incurred	(3.7)		(5.7)	
Provision released	4.8	1.1	—	(8.8)
Profit on ordinary activities before interest		32.6		20.7
Net interest payable		1.9		4.1
Profit on ordinary activities before taxation		30.7		16.6
Taxation		9.2		6.1
Profit for the financial year		21.5		10.5
Dividends		7.9		7.4
Retained profit for the financial year		13.6		3.1
Earnings per share				
—on profit for the financial year		35.3p		15.5p
—on continuing operations		34.6p		28.4p

Reconciliation of movement in shareholders' funds

	£m	£m
Retained profit for the financial year	13.6	3.1
Goodwill	(3.6)	(2.6)
Other	0.1	(0.2)
Net additions to shareholders' funds	10.1	0.3
Shareholders' funds at beginning of year	77.5	77.2
Shareholders' funds at end of year	87.6	77.5

Statement of total recognized gains and losses

There were no material recognized gains and losses other than the profit for the current and previous financial years.

Figure 6.1 *Published group profit and loss account for John Menzies plc*

The profit and loss account in Figure 6.1 discloses turnover and profit broken down between continuing and discontinued operations. It also discloses an exceptional profit from the release of part of a provision previously set up in connection with the discontinued US operation.

The increase in shareholders' funds during the year of £10.1m is detailed in the reconciliation statement. Retained profit for the year of £13.6m is offset by a net write-off of £3.6m goodwill on acquisitions/disposals, to give an increase of £10.0m. To this is added an increase of £0.1m in the currency reserve, making a total change of £10.1m in shareholders' funds.

All material recognized gains and losses are contained in the profit and loss accounts for the two years, so there are no further entries in the formal statement of total recognized gains and losses.

EARNINGS PER SHARE

One intention of FRS 3 was to provide users of financial accounts with a more detailed analysis of the figures so that attention was not just concentrated on the bottom line figure of earnings per share. FRS 3 effectively abolished so-called 'extraordinary items' which previously had been excluded from the earnings per share calculation. This had led to accusations of companies massaging their earnings per share by putting closure and restructuring costs against this heading.

It is arguable that a group of companies will be incurring such costs on a continuing basis as it shapes itself to changing demand and environment. If so, they are a valid charge against profits and should be taken into account in the calculation of earnings per share.

One consequence of this is that the earnings per share figure is now likely to be more volatile than before.

FRS 3 does allow companies to disclose an additional earnings per share figure, with certain provisos. It must be based on a level of profit different to the profit for the financial year; it must not be given more prominence than the FRS 3 figure based on the profit for the financial year; it should be used consistently over time; and a reconciliation of the two earnings per share figures is required.

You will see in the John Menzies profit and loss account above that two earnings per share figures were quoted. The first figure is the profit for the financial year of £21.5m less preference share dividends of £1.9m to give earnings attributable to ordinary shareholders of £19.6m, which is then divided by 55.55m shares to give an earnings per share of 35.3p. This meets the official requirement of FRS 3.

The second earnings per share figure quoted is based on the profit attributable to ordinary shareholders from continuing operations only. This can act as a benchmark for measuring future years' performance when the discontinued activities, by definition, are no longer included. In John Menzies' case this slightly reduces the earnings per share based on the profit for the financial year, because of the clawback of the prior year provision relating to a discontinued activity.

The FRS 3 definition of earnings per share embraces *all* realized gains and losses. Because of this, certain users of accounting statements might have difficulty in comparing performance between companies. This could occur where exceptional profits and losses of a capital nature, for example subsidiary companies or fixed assets, distort a particular company's performance compared to another company in terms of the underlying trading activity.

The Institute of Investment Management and Research (IIMR) has come up with a 'headline earnings' definition to solve this problem[2] (see also an article in *Accountancy*[3]). This bases the calculation of earnings per share on all the trading items in the profit and loss account but excludes any capital items. The *Financial Times* is using the IIMR headline earnings in its share service reporting, as is Extel Financial.

CURRENT COST ACCOUNTING

Current cost accounting relates to a system of financial reporting that adjusts for the effects of changing price levels in the financial statements. Current cost accounting (CCA) contrasts with historical cost accounting (HCA), which makes no adjustment for inflation other than an occasional revaluation of specific fixed assets such as land and buildings.

The whole topic is little commented on in company financial reports, which concentrate on reporting financial results in historical cost terms. This conveniently ignores the effects of inflation, which generally speaking make worse reading in profit terms, but better reading in terms of asset values.

Exceptions to this criticism are found with privatized utilities. Their accounts are subject to close scrutiny by their regulators, who demand both historical and current cost information. Consequently, it is in these utilities' accounts that you will find current cost statements, usually in the notes after the historical cost accounts have been presented. British Gas plc is one of a very few companies which presents its mainstream accounts in current cost terms, and always has done, relegating the historical cost accounts to the accompanying notes to the accounts.

In 1980, after much prompting by government following a period of high inflation, the Accounting Standards Committee introduced SSAP 16, entitled *Current Cost Accounting*. This required listed companies and large private companies to clarify the effects of inflation on both the profit earned in the year and on the value of the assets at the year-end.

Unfortunately, the system of adjustments introduced did not gain wide support outside the accounting profession. The Inland Revenue continued to tax historical cost profits; trade unions were suspicious of any system that made companies appear less profitable and therefore less able to afford pay increases; and investors did not fully understand the two different sets of accounts with which they were now faced. So the system fell into disuse through lack of interest, and most companies continued to present only historical cost accounts in their annual reports.

It is useful, however, for a manager to understand the effects of inflation on a business entity, and the reasoning behind the various adjustments that accountants recommended in that defunct standard. Although inflation is at a low rate at the time of writing, the cumulative effect of 3 per cent inflation for, say, ten years is considerable. Those companies still producing current cost accounting information do so with reference to this old standard, or some variant of it. At the time of writing, the Accounting Standards Board is considering this whole problem area of valuation again.

The profit and loss account is geared to the interests of shareholders and the bottom line is the profit after tax, interest and all other expenses have been allowed. If this profit were to be wholly distributed, even in low inflationary times, the company would be partly distributing capital and not just profit. This is because it would not be retaining enough profit to keep the real value of its capital intact. Looking at it from a shareholder's point of view, the true profit is that which makes allowance for the effect of inflation on a company's finances. This requires the following adjustments to historical cost profit:

■ *depreciation adjustment*—extra depreciation to that already provided in the historical profit and loss account is needed when depreciation is based on the current value of the assets rather than their original cost;
■ *cost of sales adjustment*—extra finance is needed to replace stocks at prices ruling at the time of sale;
■ *monetary working capital adjustment*—extra working capital is needed to give increased credit to customers because of inflation. This is offset partly by increased credit obtained from suppliers as their invoice values also rise with inflation.

In reality, shareholders may not have to bear all of these extra costs on their own, because most companies are financed with a mix of shareholders' funds and borrowings. The cost to be borne by shareholders is therefore the proportion of the above adjustments that their shareholders' funds represent to the total capital. This apportioning of the three extra costs above, caused by inflation, is referred to as the 'gearing adjustment' and is the fourth adjustment to historical cost profit.

At this stage it might be useful to examine British Gas plc's profit and loss accounts under both current and historical cost accounting systems, before going on to reconcile and explain the differences. The information in Figure 6.2 is extracted from the company's published accounts for the year ended 31 December 1993.[4]

The loss for the financial period is shown to be considerably higher at £533m in current cost terms than it is in historical cost terms at £285m. A reconciliation statement is provided by British Gas plc in their directors' report and accounts, as shown in Figure 6.3.

Group profit and loss accounts

	CCA 1993 (£m)	HCA 1993 (£m)
Turnover—continuing operations	10386	10386
Operating costs excluding exceptional charges	(9013)	(8702)
Restructuring costs	(1650)	(1650)
Environmental costs	(33)	(33)
Total operating costs	(10696)	(10385)
Operating profit/(loss)—continuing operations	(310)	1
Loss on sale of exploration asset—continuing operations	(46)	(46)
Profit on sale of fixed assets—continuing operations	5	7
Loss on ordinary activities before gearing adjustment and net interest	(351)	(38)
Gearing adjustment	65	N/A
Net interest	(357)	(357)
Share of profits less losses of associated undertakings	30	30
Loss on ordinary activities before taxation	(613)	(365)
Taxation on loss on ordinary activities	77	77
Loss on ordinary activities after taxation	(536)	(288)
Minority shareholders' interest	3	3
Loss for the financial period	(533)	(285)

Figure 6.2 *Published group profit and loss accounts for British Gas plc*

Reconciliation of historical and current cost losses

	1993 £m
Current cost loss on ordinary activities before taxation	(613)
Current cost adjustments:	
Cost of sales adjustment	12
Monetary working capital adjustment	48
Supplementary depreciation	251
Profit on sale of tangible fixed assets	2
Gearing adjustment	(65)
	248
Historical cost loss on ordinary activities before taxation	(365)

Figure 6.3 *Reconciliation of British Gas plc group CCA and HCA losses*

Four of the five adjustments are as explained earlier. The profit on the sale of tangible fixed assets adjustment is because the amount is £2m more in historical cost terms than in current cost terms. Presumably this is because the asset value was higher in current cost terms, so the profit on sale was less. This can be seen in Figure 6.2 where the two profit figures of £5m and £7m are shown alongside each other.

The other effect of inflation is on the asset values, primarily fixed assets, which show up in the balance sheet statement. Under current cost accounting, assets are revalued each year using specific price indices rather than a general price index. The comparative balance sheets for British Gas plc are given in Figure 6.4.

Balance sheets as at 31 December 1993

	CCA	HCA
	£m	£m
Fixed assets	25559	13646
Current assets	4636	4636
Creditors (amounts falling due within one year)	(3904)	(3904)
Net current assets	732	732
Total assets less current liabilities	26291	14378
Creditors (amounts falling due after more than one year)	(4197)	(4197)
Provisions for liabilities and charges	(2565)	(2565)
Net assets	19529	7616
Capital and reserves:		
British Gas shareholders' funds	19124	7211
Minority shareholders' interest	405	405
	19529	7616

Figure 6.4 *British Gas plc summary group balance sheets*

The difference between the two statements is reflected in the first line when the value of fixed assets is shown to be £11,913m more on a current cost basis than on a historical cost basis. This same difference also reflects in the total assets less current liabilities line and in the British Gas shareholders' funds.

When assets are revalued up or down, the change in value is placed in a *revaluation reserve*. This is a non-distributable reserve that forms part of shareholders' funds along with retained profits, other reserves and issued share capital.

THE VALUATION OF INTANGIBLE ASSETS

The struggle to find a definitive method to value tangible fixed assets, with a choice between historical and current cost approaches or some compromise between the two, is of long standing. Equally perplexing is the problem of how to value intangible assets in financial reporting, which centres on the two assets of goodwill and brands in particular.

Goodwill

Internally generated goodwill is not recognized in financial reporting at the time of writing. This is not to say that it has no value, but that whatever value it has is not recognized in the financial accounting statements.

The treatment of purchased goodwill is of course a different story, as a price can be identified for its acquisition. Even here the story is not straightforward. A fair value has to be established for the assets and liabilities acquired. Any excess purchase price over this fair value is counted as purchased goodwill. However, in determining fair values some companies have been including the cost of reorganization to make the two businesses fit together, so reducing the fair value and increasing the purchased goodwill element. This avoids charging the profit and loss account with these reorganization costs in later years, so protecting their earnings per share. But what happens to purchased goodwill including these reorganization costs?

Normal practice in the UK is that purchased goodwill is written off to reserves at the time of acquisition, thus avoiding any effect on the profit and loss account as only the balance sheet value of shareholders' funds is affected. The alternative allowed is that purchased goodwill is treated as an intangible asset and written off to the profit and loss account over a number of years. This latter approach will reduce future years' earnings per share while the former method will not.

It is interesting to note that the International Accounting Standards Committee, in its revised standard IAS 22, does not allow the immediate write-off of purchased goodwill. It requires such goodwill to be included in the balance sheet (or capitalized) and written off to the yearly profit and loss account over a five-year period, unless a longer life, up to a maximum 20 years, can be justified.

However, in the UK companies are now required to charge purchased goodwill to the profit and loss account at the time of disposal or closure of the business acquired. Therefore, writing off all purchased goodwill to reserves at the time of acquisition is not as attractive an option as it was.

At the end of 1993, the Accounting Standards Board issued its discussion paper on *Goodwill and Intangible Assets.*[5] In it, four methods of accounting for purchased goodwill were identified, of which Board members favoured two. The four methods are:

■ *capitalization and write-off over a predetermined life*—a maximum finite life of, say, 20 years is proposed, with a yearly review of the carrying value;

■ *capitalization and annual review*—the yearly write-off is determined by a review of the carrying value, and may be a zero charge;

■ *immediate write-off*—purchased goodwill is immediately written off in full to reserves;

■ *separate write-off reserve*—purchased goodwill is immediately written off to a separate write-off reserve.

The favoured approaches by Board members are a combination of the first two methods, with the annual review approach implemented after a period of, say, 20 years. The second favoured method is the last one—creating a separate write-off reserve which remains intact until the acquired business is sold or closed down.

Brands

The Accounting Standards Board discussion paper argued that the purchase of other intangible assets closely resemble purchased goodwill and that most such purchases should be subsumed within it for financial reporting purposes.

This leaves internally generated brands as an issue, although mixed opinions again abound, perhaps illustrated by the takeover of Rank Hovis McDougall by Tomkins. The former was a keen advocate of brand values being included in balance sheets and practised what it preached. After the takeover in 1992, Tomkins proceeded to write off the £459m brand value in RHM's balance sheet because it had not been its practice to include such intangibles in its own balance sheet.

If you are interested in brand valuation techniques, you will find an article by Mullen[6] very helpful. She identifies three principal methods to arrive at the cash flows or profits that can be attributed to a specific intangible asset, not exclusively limited to brands:

■ *Premium profits*—the additional profit accruing to the owner of the intangible asset compared with a similar business without such asset. These future sums are then capitalized to a lump sum value, possibly using a discounted cash flow technique as explained in Chapter 10.

- *Residual value*—the business owning the intangible asset is valued twice; once on the basis of the profits or cash flows including those derived from the asset, next on the basis that it did not own the intangible asset. The difference between the two business valuations is the value of the intangible asset in question.
- *Relief from royalties/royalties forgone*—this approach calculates the yearly royalties that would have to be paid if the owner of the intangible asset was not the owner and had to pay royalties. Alternatively, the royalties forgone are the royalties that could have been earned each year if use of the intangible asset had been licensed out. In both cases the yearly stream has to be capitalized into a lump-sum value.

References

1. John Menzies plc (1993) *Annual report and accounts*, Edinburgh.
2. The Institute of Investment Management and Research, Kent (1993) *The definition of headline earnings.*
3. (1993) 'Happy ending for addicted analysts', *Accountancy*, October.
4. British Gas plc (1993) *Annual report and accounts*, London.
5. Accounting Standards Board (1993) *Goodwill and intangible assets*, discussion paper.
6. Mullen, M (1993) 'How to value intangibles', *Accountancy*, November.

Part Two
Management accounting

You will not find financial accounting statements of much help in the day-to-day running of your part of the business, although a knowledge and understanding of them is vital to put your decision making in context.

This second part of the book aims to give you tools and techniques to assist you in the crucial management roles of financial planning and decision making. Very many decisions which managers take are based on financial data. Knowing what information to ask for and how to use it is an essential requirement for all managers.

First we need an introductory chapter on all the different ways of analysing costs, before we cover pricing, short-term decisions, budgetary control and long-term investment appraisal.

7

Costing

osting is really the 'nitty-gritty' of finance—it is the detailed analysis of expenditure going into the profit and loss account. It is the analysis of costs to products or services, to departments and to specific time periods. As a manager you are unlikely to make more than an occasional reference to the company profit and loss account, but you are likely to be using cost information on a regular basis. There are many costing terms so we need to learn a little bit of the language before discussing the practical uses of costing techniques in this and subsequent chapters.

Costs can be analysed objectively in terms of where they are to be charged. This can be to:

■ a cost unit, and/or
■ a cost centre.

A *cost unit* is any job, product, contract or service provided for a customer, whilst a *cost centre* is a physical location within an organization, typically a functional department or a section where you work.

Costs can also be analysed subjectively by a description of the labour, material and expenses consumed, grouped under *direct* or *indirect* cost headings:

■ direct labour;
■ direct materials;
■ direct expenses;
■ indirect labour;
■ indirect materials;
■ indirect expenses.

A *direct cost* is one that has a specific identity with a cost unit or cost centre. An indirect cost has no such relationship and has to be apportioned over cost units, or cost centres, in what may sometimes be an arbitrary manner. Each item of direct and indirect cost is identified by its own unique code number.

COST CODES

A *cost code* is a numbering device that turns a written description of costs into a series of numbers or, in the case of an alphanumeric code, a mixture of numbers and letters. Cost code numbers, often called the *chart of accounts*, identify:

- which cost centre incurred the cost;
- what resource has been consumed;
- to which cost unit the cost is to be charged.

A typical cost code structure, made up of three blocks to cater for the above information, could look like Figure 7.1. Your organization might put the blocks in a different sequence, or use more or less digits in any of the blocks, but it should be comparable in broad purpose and outline.

Cost centre number	Describing number	Cost unit number
XXX	XXX	XXXXX
Identification number for business unit and department.	Each detailed cost, asset, liability and revenue item has a separate account code.	Each job, batch, contract or order has a unique number.

Figure 7.1 *Typical cost code structure*

Use of computers

Accountants receive information about costs from managers and supervisors in their organization who forward timesheets, invoices, goods received notes and stores issue notes. These may be coded at source or coded later by the accounting staff. Direct costs can be coded to both cost units and cost centres, while indirect costs can only be coded to cost centres. Knowing which department indirect costs originated in, helps with the apportionment of these overheads at a later stage. The wider use of computers to process financial data is shown in Figure 7.2.

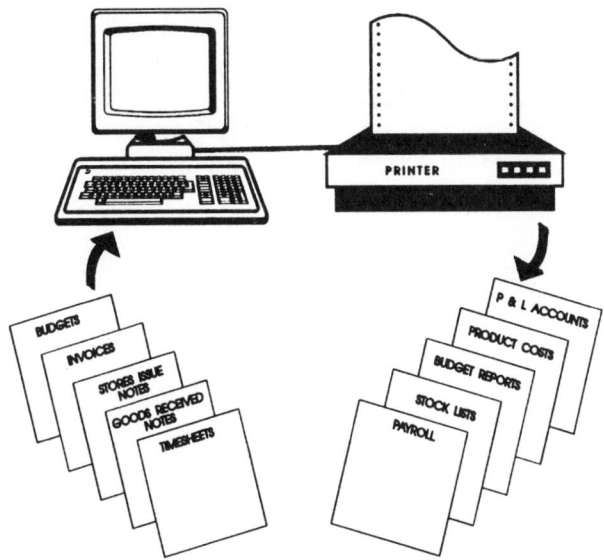

Figure 7.2 *Using a computer to process financial data*

The resources firms consume consist of three basic elements:

■ *labour*—the cost of employing people in both direct and indirect activities;
■ *materials*—the cost of materials and components used in production/service activities;
■ *expenses*—the cost of bought-in services, possibly directly chargeable to cost units but mainly overheads like rates, heating and insurance, chargeable to cost centres.

LABOUR REMUNERATION

The remuneration paid to employees can be based on the time worked, on output achieved, or on some combination of the two. The main types of payment system are:

■ *time-based system*—pays a basic hourly rate for normal hours, an enhanced rate thereafter;
■ *measured day work*—pays high basic rates for meeting high-quality, high-effort targets;

- *incentive scheme/piecework*—relates pay to output with safeguards built in;
- *premium bonus system*—pays normal hourly rates plus a bonus for any time saved.

Regardless of payment method, the cost of direct workers is charged directly to the cost units on which they work, enhanced by employer's contributions to National Insurance, holidays and pension schemes. Similarly, the pay of indirect workers can be charged to the cost centres where they work and later apportioned to the cost units benefiting from that cost centre's services. This overhead recovery process is discussed later.

MATERIAL COSTS

Firms may hold stocks of materials/components in their stores for issue at a later date. The purchase and subsequent issue of these materials need to be documented at various stages to ensure that volumes and values are known and charged to the correct cost units and cost centres.
Typical documents are:

- *purchase requisitions*—raised internally as soon as the reorder point is triggered;
- *purchase orders*—sent to selected suppliers with specified delivery times;
- *goods received notes (GRNs)*—matched with purchase order;
- *goods returned notes*—raised only if goods need to be returned to suppliers;
- *suppliers' invoices*—checked against GRNs before payment is made;
- *stores requisitions*—when duly authorized, the only means of obtaining stores issues;
- *stock records*—kept manually or on computer to record all receipts and issues.

Pricing stores issues

It might not seem obvious that materials can be charged out from store at more than one price. For example, a material could be priced at its most recent purchase price or at the oldest price paid for any of that item currently in stock. The full range of possibilities are:

- *first in first out (FIFO)*—a popular method that issues oldest materials first at old prices;

- *last in first out (LIFO)*—popular in the US but not acceptable to the Inland Revenue in UK;
- *standard price*—all similar materials are held in stock and issued at the one price;
- *weighted average price*—this is a compromise between FIFO and LIFO systems.

Example

A firm bought 200 units of material at 60p per unit in May and a further 400 units at 50p in August. The standard purchase price specified for this material is 60p. The cost of an issue of 300 units in September and the value of the stock remaining under each pricing system is:

Pricing method	Calculations	Issue value	Stock value
FIFO	(200× 60p) + (100 × 50p)	£170	£150
LIFO	300 × 50p	£150	£170
Standard	300 × 60p	£180	£180
Average	300 × 53.33p	£160	£160

Over the whole life span of any one company there will be no difference between these four methods of pricing stores issues and the total profit made. However, this is not true when we consider a short time period like a month or a year in the life of a company. Clearly, the profit made in any period will differ according to which method of stores pricing is used, as will the remaining stock valuation.

The FIFO method of stores pricing flatters profit when material prices are rising, with profit being adversely affected when material prices are falling. These effects are more muted under the weighted average price system. The standard price is the most realistic provided it is updated for market price changes. Under this system any variance on buying price is charged to the profit and loss account immediately and stock values are shown in the balance sheet at standard prices.

Once materials have been priced, direct materials can be charged out to cost units using the relevant cost unit code. Indirect materials are charged to the cost centre incurring them and later apportioned to cost units under the overhead recovery system discussed later.

EXPENSES

Direct expenses, for example the hire of equipment, can be allocated directly to the cost unit concerned in much the same way as direct labour and direct materials. Indirect expenses have no such direct link and must be accumulated in the cost centres where they arise along with indirect labour and materials. All these indirect costs are recovered by absorbing them into cost units.

OVERHEAD RECOVERY

Overheads and indirect costs mean the same thing. Overheads are just as necessary as direct costs even if they are sometimes referred to as non-productive costs. Sales representatives are just as important as production workers for the obvious reason that without a sale, production becomes totally unnecessary.

From a costing point of view, overheads pose a challenge. If we are to work out the total cost of any cost unit we need to include a share of the indirect costs as well as its direct costs. This total cost sometimes forms the basis for price fixing when an element of profit is added.

The question posed for accountants and managers is—how much overhead should be charged to different product lines and to each cost unit? There are three broad answers:

- use a global overhead recovery method;
- use a departmental overhead recovery method;
- use an activity based overhead recovery method.

Global overhead recovery

A local garage estimates that its total overheads for the coming year will amount to £200,000. It also estimates that rechargeable hours will come to 20,000 in the year. The overhead charge (recovery rate) is £10 per hour. A job lasting two hours will be charged out at the cost of the direct labour and materials plus a further £20 to cover overheads. This can be seen diagrammatically in Figure 7.3.

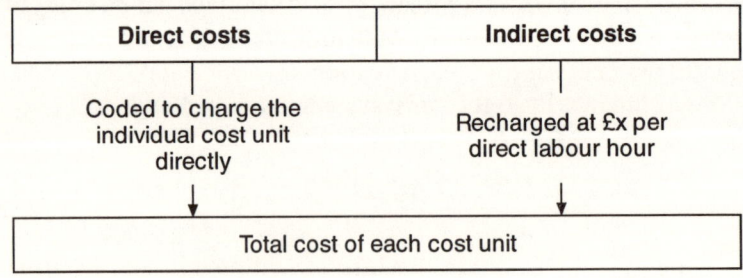

Figure 7.3 *Global method of overhead recovery*

The global overhead recovery rate may seem fair when all work is similar in nature, is labour intensive and uses the same equipment. It may seem less than fair to some customers who find out that overheads include depreciation on an expensive piece of equipment that was not needed for their particular repairs. On a wider scale, this can lead to cross-subsidization, incorrect pricing and loss of profit.

Having pointed out this system's disadvantages, it is still widely used in small organizations ranging from engineering companies to professionals like architects and solicitors. In many cases it is a reasonably fair method of recharging overheads relating to the provision of goods and services that are labour intensive in nature. The cost of collecting and analysing overheads to operate a more sophisticated system might outweigh the benefits to these kinds of organization and not lead to substantially different results.

Departmental overhead recovery

Larger firms with diversified products and more diverse production or operations systems find the global approach to overheads inappropriate. They cannot afford to undercharge some products, so gaining market share on less profitable lines, and overcharge other products, so losing market share on what in reality are more profitable lines.

For this reason they channel all overheads into their relevant cost centres where they arise. Any cost centres providing a service to other operational cost centres have all their overheads recharged to them on the basis of the amount of service provided. All overheads are now in operational cost centres and each is recharged only to those cost units passing through its cost centre. In this way equity is established between different cost units. This can be seen diagrammatically in Figure 7.4.

This method of overhead apportionment to cost units was and is widely practised by medium and large organizations. However, in the late 1980s its validity was questioned by Professors Kaplan and Cooper of Harvard Business School.

They argued that when a company produces a diversity of low-volume and high-volume products, the traditional route to overhead apportionment, and hence product costs, distorts reality. This led to the birth of activity-based costing (ABC) which, while still in its infancy, has generated enormous interest and experimentation in service as well as in manufacturing industries.

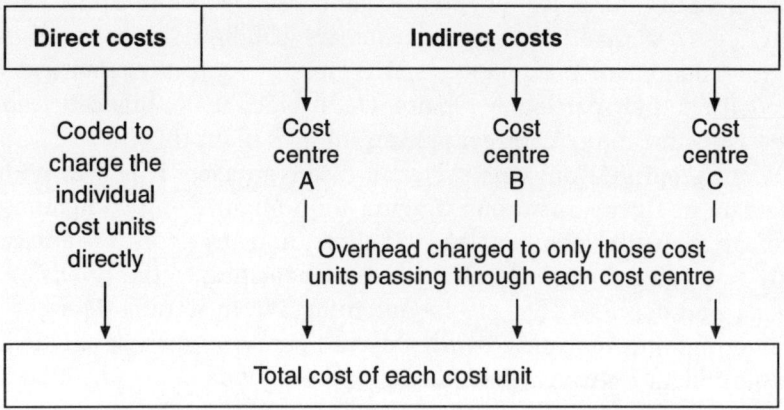

Figure 7.4 *Departmental overhead recovery method*

Activity based costing (ABC)

Consider the case of two factories producing the same total volume of similar products. One factory concentrates on mass production, while the other factory customizes its products to individual customer requirements, resulting in many short production runs.

The support services for the two factories will obviously differ in response to the different needs. The second factory will have more varied material ordering, stores handling, production scheduling, production set-ups, quality inspections and similar requirements, than will be the case for the first factory.

If the cost of these support services is charged to individual products *based on their production volumes*, this will distort the real costs incurred by each product. Low-volume products will attract low support service overheads because the real costs incurred by short runs are not identified. This will distort product costs and pricing between products in one factory and between competing factories. High-volume products will bear more than their fair share of these support service overheads, even though they were caused more by low-volume products.

The starting point for implementing ABC is to identify the main activities in an organization. These are unlikely to coincide wholly with functionally based departments and sections. Each production/ operation/support activity will form a cost pool or cost centre of its own.

The next stage is to identify the cause(s) of each activity's cost. Such causes are known as 'cost drivers'. For example, when dealing with overheads relating to a purchasing activity, appropriate cost drivers might be the number of suppliers and the number of orders placed. Cost drivers need to be found for each and every activity.

The third stage is to collect overheads into separate cost pools for each activity, very much akin to collecting overheads by departmental cost centres in a traditional overhead allocation system.

Finally, overheads are charged to products according to the demands made on each activity as measured by the number of transactions for its cost driver. The ABC approach is illustrated in Figure 7.5.

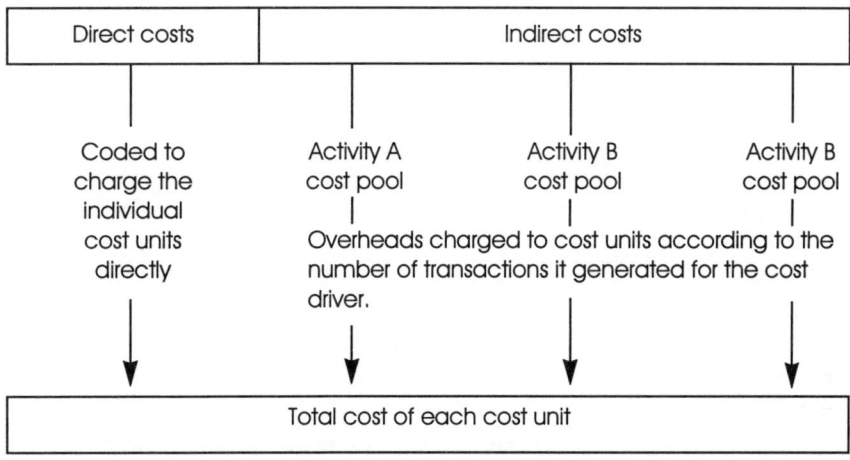

Figure 7.5 *ABC method of overhead recovery*

If you want to know more about ABC, try reading Johnson and Kaplan's book *Relevance lost*[1], or some of the many articles on this topic found in CIMA's monthly *Management Accounting* magazine.

We can now see how the total cost of any product or service is built up. Direct labour, direct materials and direct expenses can all be coded with the relevant job number in the coding system. Indirect labour, indirect materials and indirect expenses have to be shared out over the cost units in a way that does not favour one cost unit at the expense of another. This is performed using a global, departmental or activity-based overhead allocation system. The total cost of each cost unit results from the sum of all direct costs plus a share of apportioned overheads. This leads us into a discussion of *full cost pricing*.

FULL COST PRICING

All organizations need to know the total cost of each product or service they provide to their customers for a number of reasons, although we only concentrate on the last one:

■ to value stocks and work in progress in the balance sheet;
■ to determine the cost of sales in the profit and loss account;
■ to determine the profit made at any particular selling price;
■ to compare actual costs with predetermined standard costs;
■ to fix selling prices based on the total cost, although other influences are important.

The costing procedure for working out the selling price of any product or service is the same, irrespective of whether it takes place before or after the work is completed. This procedure is referred to as 'absorption costing' by accountants, or less technically as 'full cost' or 'total cost pricing' by others.

Absorption costing

The term absorption costing was chosen to describe the approach whereby products each absorb a share of all the overhead costs in addition to their direct costs. We can therefore say:

Selling price = Direct costs + Share of overheads + Profit

The precise methods used, and overhead recovery rates charged, vary from one organization to another, and one industry to another. Below is an example of full cost pricing using a departmental overhead recovery basis.

Profit margins vary from industry to industry and in the way they are achieved. The retail trade may add a percentage mark-up to the cost of the goods sold, thereby aiming for a set gross margin. Other industries target the net margin after due recovery of a share of the overheads. Typical profit margins can be found from data published by:

■ trade associations;
■ credit agencies, eg Dun & Bradstreet;
■ business monitoring organizations, eg Extel (available in large libraries)
■ interfirm comparisons.

Example

The following details have been assembled to work out the price for a job in response to a customer's request:

Direct materials: 7.5 kilos at £10.50 per kilo

Direct labour:	Department	Hours	Rate per hour
	Machine shop	2.0	£8
	Assembly dept	1.0	£6
	Packing shop	0.2	£5

Overheads: These are recovered by means of separate hourly recovery rates for each department and then by adding a 25 per cent oncost to cover selling and administrative costs plus an element of profit.

The annual budgets for the three departments are:

Department	Hours	Overheads	Hourly rate
Machine shop	1000	£50,000	£50.00
Assembly dept	1500	£22,500	£15.00
Packing shop	800	£26,000	£32.50

The price quotation can be prepared as follows:

		£	£
Direct materials: 7.5 kilos at £10.50			78.75
Direct labour: 2 hours at £8		16.00	
1 hour at £6		6.00	
0.2 hours at £5		1.00	23.00
Overheads: 2 hours at £50		100.00	
1 hour at £15		15.00	
0.2 hours at £32.50		6.50	121.50
Total works cost:			223.25
25 per cent oncost for selling and administration costs and profit			55.81
Selling price to quote to customer			279.06

A survey of large manufacturing and service companies in the late 1980s by Mills and Sweeting[2] showed that cost-related pricing methods were the most popular with about 70 per cent of the respondents. A similar proportion also selected full/absorption costing as the primary cost method used.

In a later survey of management accounting practices in UK manufacturing organizations by Drury et al,[3] it was found that cost-plus pricing was used selectively by 84 per cent of respondents, with 77 per cent often or always using either total manufacturing cost or total cost, 50 per cent often or always using variable manufacturing cost or total variable cost, and 32 per cent combining the total and variable approaches. The proportion of respondents who often or always compared product costs with market-determined selling prices was as high as 88 per cent.

The conclusion is that most profit-seeking companies do not stick rigidly to prices determined by total costs. Companies use absorption costing as a long-term guide to what they need to sell at to earn a reasonable rate of return, or they use 'target costing' to drive down product costs to a level that will earn a satisfactory margin on the target selling price.

In the short term, many companies, perhaps your own organization included, trim their prices to suit market conditions. This move is often disguised by using a price/discount formula. In this way they come nearer to the contribution approach to pricing espoused by marginal costing.

Customer profitability analysis

In the past, management accountants' attention has perhaps focused on product profitability, with insufficient regard to the profitability of different types of customer. Where sales all go through the same channel of distribution to the same market, with no predominant customers, an analysis of customer profitability may yield little benefit.

Where sales are channelled through different markets—retail, wholesale and industrial—or where one or two major customers account for a substantial part of total sales, an analysis of the profitability of each market and each major customer may prove enlightening. Large customers are not necessarily the most profitable ones if, for example, they place large numbers of small orders and/or demand non-standard products or services.

An activity-based approach will help in channelling customer-related overheads to customers in a meaningful way, rather than the more arbitrary traditional manner. The resulting profitability analysis will help decision making on eliminating overheads which do not add value and, in the extreme, on eliminating customers or a channel of distribution. If you wish to read more on customer profitability analysis, try articles by Connelly and Ashworth[4] and/or Smith.[5]

COSTING METHODS

In practice it may not be quite so simple to work out the cost (and possible selling price) of a cost unit. Some cost units result from continuous processes rather than discrete production, so that a unit cost can only be found on an average basis. Some large construction projects last a number of years before their completion and may or may not be capable of division into a number of smaller cost units.

For these and other reasons, some industries have developed their own costing methods to cope with the complexities and peculiarities of their situation. These costing methods are usually variations of the two broad types of costing, ie job costing or process costing:

- *Job costing*—used for unique, bespoke products, repairs and services where each order is allocated a unique job number to accumulate all its costs.
- *Batch costing*—where uniform products are produced in batches and each batch is allocated its own job number.
- *Contract costing*—for large engineering fabrications, eg an oil rig or a new road. A job number, or series of numbers for parts of the total contract, are used to accumulate all the contract costs including overheads specifically incurred at the contract site.
- *Process costing*—where production is a continuous process 24 hours a day. Costs are accumulated for each process but the unit cost can only be found by averaging total costs in a period of time by the total output during that same period.
- *Service costing*—any large, one-off service will be treated as job costing, but repetitive services are similar to process costing.

COST CONTROL

The purpose of cost control is to monitor past unit costs with a view to improving future performance. This monitoring can be done by comparing the latest actual unit costs with one or more of the following:

- previous unit costs;
- predetermined estimates or standard costs;
- competitors' unit costs.

This can be thought of as a control cycle of four sequential stages that repeats itself after each cycle is completed, as in Figure 7.6.

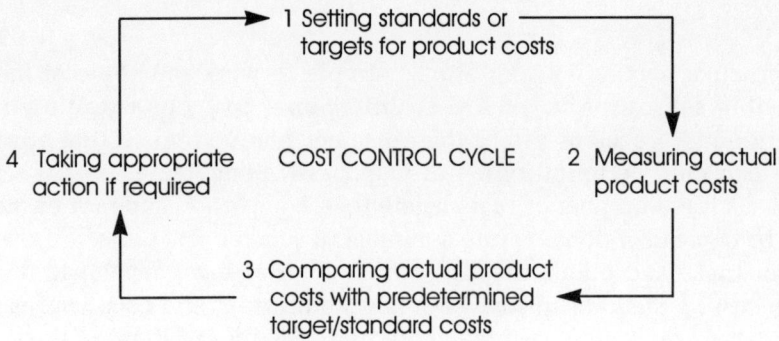

Figure 7.6 *Cost control cycle*

STANDARD COSTING

The scientific management technique of standard costing is said to bring benefits in budgeting and performance measurement, motivation and cost control to companies making mass-produced articles. It involves:

- setting resource and efficiency levels using scientific management techniques in preference to past data on labour and material costs;
- working out the standard cost for labour, materials and overheads for each product. This should be on a realistic and attainable basis as opposed to *ideal* standards which are unattainable and therefore demotivating. Easily attainable standards with built-in slack will also not provide the motivation required;
- setting standard selling prices for each product;
- computing the variances between actual costs and standard costs;
- analysing the variances into their root causes and investigating significant amounts so that time is not wasted on relatively small variances.

When an actual product cost is compared with its standard cost, some difference is likely to result. This difference is called a 'variance' in accounting. In the following example, when a batch of these metal boxes is made, it is unlikely that the actual cost will be exactly as laid down in the standard specification. After identifying the variance on each element of cost, standard costing goes on to analyse the variances further into their root causes. Basically there are two main types of variance—those relating to *price* and those relating to *volume*, as shown in the second example overleaf.

Example

Standard cost specification for batch of 100 metal boxes

	Quantity	Unit price	Standard cost £
Materials: Metal strip—Grade A	40 kg	£25 per kg	1000.00
—Packing carton	1	£2.50 each	2.50
			1002.50
Labour: Operator 1	4 hours	£6 per hour	24.00
Operator 2	8 hours	£5 per hour	40.00
Operator 3	1 hour	£4 per hour	4.00
			68.00
Overheads: standard allowance	100 units	£3.20 per unit	320.00
Total standard cost			1390.50
Standard profit			152.00
Standard selling price			1542.50

Example

Referring back to the standard cost specification, let us assume 20 batches of metal boxes were made, using 900 kg of metal bought in at £23 per kg. The total material cost variance is the difference between the actual cost and the standard cost. This can be either adverse (A) if it leads to less profit or favourable (F) if it means more profit than expected:

Actual cost	Standard cost	Material cost variance
900 kg × £23 = £20,700	20 × 40kg × £25 = £20,000	£700 (A)

This £700 variance results from two causes and not just one. On the one hand, extra costs were incurred through using 100 kg more metal than was specified, resulting in a material usage variance of 100kg × £25 = £2500 (A). On the other hand, the firm bought the material for £2 per kg less than it expected and thus saved £2 × 900kg = £1800 (F), which is the material price variance. To summarize:

Total material cost variance	£700 (A)
Material usage variance	£2500 (A)
Material price variance	£1800 (F)
	£700 (A)

Variances for other costs, and for sales, can be similarly divided into two main types, as shown below, although it must be stressed that an even deeper analysis is possible in many industries:

Price variances:

■ material price variance;
■ labour rate variance;
■ overhead expenditure variance;
■ sales price variance.

Volume variances:

■ material usage variance;
■ labour efficiency variance;
■ overhead volume variance;
■ sales volume variance.

When a full system of standard costing is used, the variances explain why the budgeted profit was not achieved, and reconcile budgeted and actual profits in the period. The variances themselves show both the significance of and detailed reasons for actual profits differing from expectations, as shown in the example below. This allows management to home in on the cause of any problems without having to do a lot of detective work.

Example

	(F)	(A)	£
Budgeted profit for the week			7000
Variances:	(F)	(A)	
Sales price variance	900		
Sales quantity variance		700	
Material price variance	475		
Material usage variance		250	
Labour rate variance		225	
Labour efficiency variance	—	—	
Overhead expenditure variance	500		
Overhead volume variance		350	
	1875	1525	350 (F)
Actual profit for the week			£7350

This example shows that profit increased by £350 compared to what was originally expected. The causes of this extra profit are as numerous as the number of variances listed. Increases in profit of £1875 for the week were obtained via better selling prices, cheaper material buying-in prices and reduced overhead costs. However, these gains were offset by adverse variances totalling £1525 due to lower sales volume, excessive material usage, higher rates of pay and an underrecovery of overheads due to the lower sales volume.

Drury et al, in their survey of UK manufacturing organizations,[3] found that 76 per cent of their respondents used a standard costing system and a further 11 per cent had ceased to use such systems in the previous ten years. On these figures standard costing is far from dead, despite suggestions to the contrary by some other writers.

The nature of some service organizations means that standards, estimates and tenders have no relevance. These organizations can still control costs, but in a different way. One way suitable for monitoring a repetitive service, even if each operation is not totally standard, is to compare the *average cost per service* over time, making due allowance for inflation if necessary.

A further comparison can be made with similar organizations providing similar services under similar conditions. This may lead to collaboration on benchmarking (see Chapter 5), an interorganization study of the whole process of providing goods or services. Its aim is not just to control or reduce costs, but also to achieve superior performance by the study and comparison of methods and processes to effect improvements all round.

In some cases it may prove useful to compare the actual cost of a service with the selling price obtainable. If an insufficient surplus results, this may signal the case for cost reduction or obtaining a better price.

SUMMARY

This chapter has introduced you to some of the basic ideas in costing, including full cost pricing and cost control using standard costing and other comparisons. If you need to know more about these matters, try reading the authoritative text on management and cost accounting by Drury listed in the Bibliography.

The next chapter is still about costing, but takes as its theme the use of cost information for short-term decision making. We introduce *cost behaviour* relative to output levels and go on to examine *break-even analysis* and the concept of *contribution*.

References

1. Johnson, H T and Kaplan, R S (1987) *Relevance lost: the rise and fall of management accounting*, Harvard Business School Press.

2. Mills, R W and Sweeting, R (1988) *Pricing decisions in practice*, CIMA, London.

3. Drury, C, Braund, S, Osborne, P and Tayles, M (1993) A *survey of management accounting practices in UK manufacturing companies*, ACCA.

4. Connolly, T and Ashworth, G (1994) 'Managing customers for profit', *Management Accounting* (UK), April.

5. Smith, M (1993) 'Customer profitability analysis revisited', *Management Accounting* (UK), October.

8

Marginal costing

C ost information is the basis for much decision making in business today. We have already seen in the previous chapter how cost data is used both to fix prices and to control costs. We now return to costs to consider how such information can help you to make other decisions.

Typical decision making situations are:

■ how costs will behave if the level of activity changes;
■ what level of activity is needed to make a profit;
■ which product lines contribute most to profits;
■ how to choose between different operating methods;
■ how to maximize the use of scarce resources.

COST BEHAVIOUR

Marginal costing is a technique which divides costs into two categories and then uses that information in decision making. The two categories describe costs as either *fixed* or *variable* when related to the level of activity.

A fixed cost is so called because it does not vary in total when the level of activity varies. Rent and rates for an office, a shop or a factory are classic examples of fixed costs.

In contrast, a variable cost is one whose total does vary in sympathy with the level of activity. The value of direct materials used to make products and the cost of operatives' labour are typical examples of variable costs. When the level of activity increases by x per cent the total of these costs also increases by approximately x per cent. Similarly, when the level of output falls, these variable costs fall proportionately. These cost behaviours can be depicted on graphs, as we shall see later.

The similarity of variable costs to direct costs, and of fixed costs to indirect costs, is sometimes a source of confusion. They are not quite the same for a number of reasons. Direct material costs are usually also a variable cost, but this need not be true of direct labour. If a firm has a guaranteed weekly minimum wage regardless of output, then in the short term this is a fixed cost. Should all the labour force not be needed in the slightly longer term, then this direct labour cost becomes a variable cost and is normally regarded as such. The exception might be a decision on what to do with idle labour in the next few days if they are guaranteed a minimum wage. Labour then becomes a fixed cost in this short period.

Fixed costs are not necessarily synonymous with indirect costs, because there are a number of variable overhead costs. Examples of variable overheads are energy costs, quality inspection and freight charges.

If you are a car owner you may have considered the cost of keeping a car on the road. Taking miles as indicative of the level of activity, we can place the various costs of running a car into the following fixed and variable categories:

Cost	*Behaviour*
Petrol and oil	A variable cost
Tyres	A variable cost
Road fund licence	A fixed cost
Insurance	A fixed cost
Services	A variable cost
Depreciation	A mixture—but mainly a fixed cost

Having defined fixed and variable costs, we now want to see how this can help you to make a decision about using the car.

Example

Suppose you want to travel to Edinburgh city centre and can go either by train or by car. Going by rail costs, say, £25, plus a further £2 for local travel to and from the station. If you do the 200 mile return journey by car, you will incur a parking fee at Edinburgh of £3 for the day. You already own a car and do about 10,000 miles each year. All your motoring costs shown below for last year amounted to £3380:

	10,000 miles	one mile
	£	p
Depreciation	2000	20.0
Insurance	450	4.5
Road find licence	110	1.1
Servicing and tyres	220	2.2 *
Petrol and oil	600	6.0 *
Total cost	3,380	33.8

Deciding which is the cheapest way to travel should be based on the incremental or variable costs of each alternative method. It is fairly easy to see that the cost of rail travel amounts to £27, being the £25 fare plus £2 for local travel.

Not quite so easy to see is the cost of car travel. At first glance it might appear that the cost is 200 miles at 33.8p per mile plus £3 for car parking, making £70.60 in total. This is misleading because only the servicing, tyres, petrol and oil costs marked * will change as a result of this journey. The depreciation, insurance and road fund licence costs are all fixed and will not change even if this journey is made.

The incremental or marginal cost of this car journey therefore comprises only 200 miles at 8.2p* making £16.40, plus the £3 parking fee which gives a total cost by car of £19.40. This is £7.60 cheaper than the alternative of going by rail.

If you are a train user, you may have observed that British Rail makes use of marginal costing in its pricing policy, for example special low fares for off-peak travel.

COST GRAPHS

It is possible to express variable and fixed costs in the form of a diagram or graph, by plotting cost on one axis and the level of output or activity on the other. This is depicted in Figure 8.1.

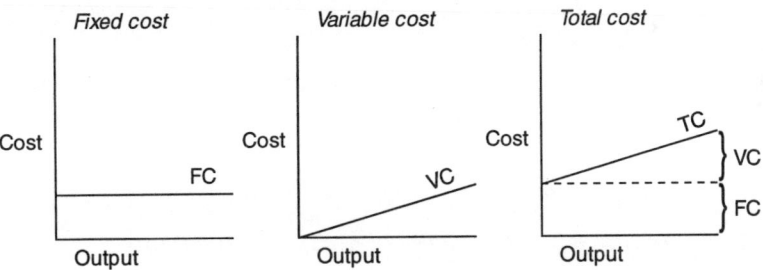

Figure 8.1 *Cost behaviour (simplistic view)*

These presentations make the basic point about the behaviour of fixed and variable costs, and therefore of total cost, but cut some corners in the process. Variable costs may not increase in the linear fashion depicted, as economies of scale have an impact when output increases from low levels. Also, when capacity constraints start to bite, diseconomies of scale may set in.

Fixed costs may also be expected to rise at intervals if output increases over a wide range. Additional rent and rates may be incurred when extra space is sought, or more administrative staff are needed when activity gets beyond the level where the existing staff can cope. This all leads to a stepped pattern of fixed costs over a wide range of activity. This is illustrated in Figure 8.2

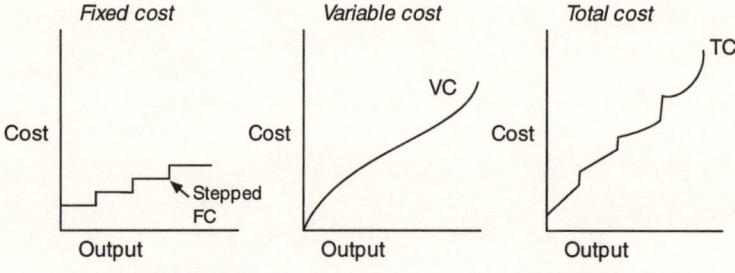

Figure 8.2 *Cost behaviour (realistic view)*

When using these charts in practice, we are normally concerned with only a small range of activity levels. This is referred to as the relevant range within which we assume that costs behave in a linear fashion, and is depicted in Figure 8.3.

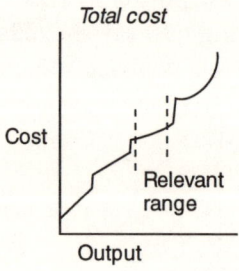

Figure 8.3 *Linear costs within the 'relevant range'*

BREAK-EVEN

We can often use simple graphs to express the relationship of total costs to output and the resulting profit or loss at different levels of activity. Such graphs are useful as an aid to decision making.

Example

You are trying to choose which of two car hire firms to patronize. Firm A offers a car at a fixed rate of £20 per day plus 20p for every mile. Firm B charges only £12 per day but its mileage rate is 30p. The two alternative situations can be drawn on one graph as in Figure 8.4, where the total cost of using each car comprises the daily fixed charge plus the mileage cost, which varies with the miles run. This is shown for daily journeys up to 120 miles.

We can conclude from the graph that firm B is the one you should use if the daily mileage is less than 80 miles, while firm A should be chosen for mileages in excess of that figure. The total cost lines for the two firms are equal at the cross-over point of 80 miles. This is referred to as the 'break-even point'.

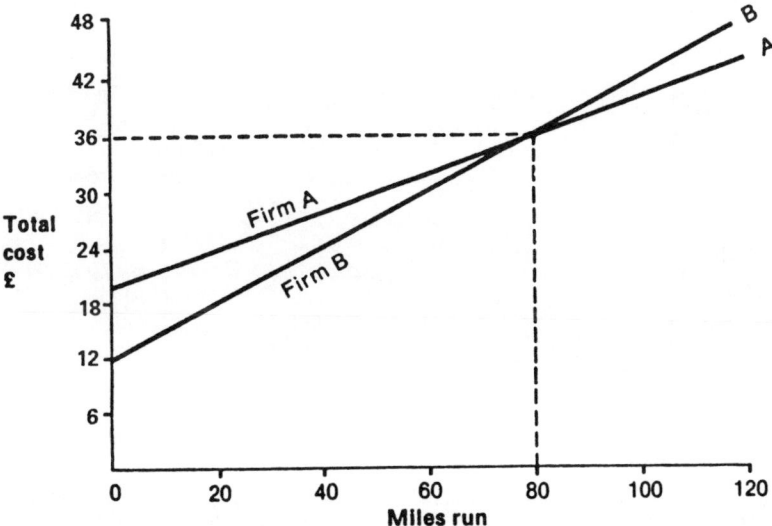

Figure 8.4 *Car hire costs*

The idea of break-even is also used by organizations to depict costs, sales revenue and output, when the break-even point is the level of output where sales revenue equals total cost. The firm makes neither a profit nor a loss at this level of output—hence the use of the term *break-even*.

Example

Suppose a firm makes only one product which sells for £10 each. The variable cost per unit is £5 and fixed costs total £75,000 per annum. Maximum capacity is 25,000 units a year, but the firm is currently achieving only 80 per cent of capacity. Figure 8.5 shows this information in the form of a break-even chart.

Break-even is reached when sales of 15,000 units for £150,000 just equal total costs of £150,000. Output of less than 15,000 units results in a loss, while a greater output makes a profit. The size of profit or loss at any output can be read off the break-even chart at a glance, being the vertical distance between the sales revenue line and the total cost line.

Also illustrated on the graph is the 'margin of safety' which represents the proportionate fall in output which can take place before a loss is incurred. In this example, the present level of 20,000 units can fall by 25 per cent to only 15,000 units before a loss would result. The margin of safety is therefore 25 per cent.

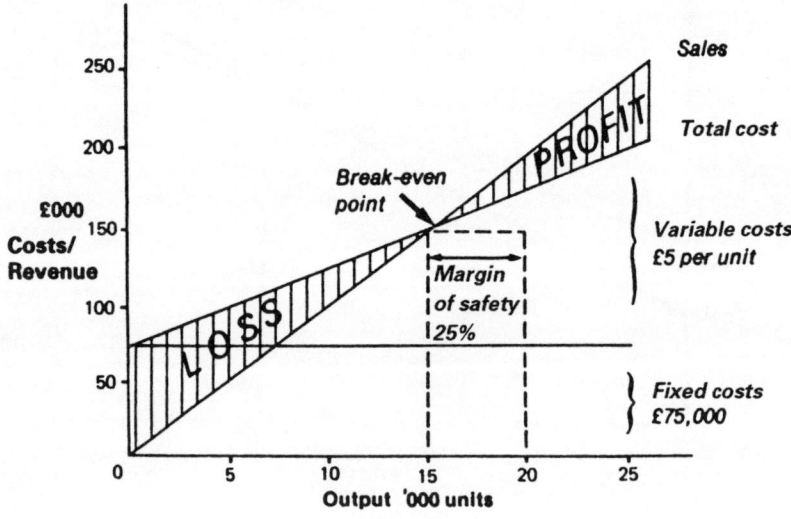

Figure 8.5 *Break-even chart*

Although costs have been identified here as being either fixed or variable, in practice there may be some costs which are a mixture. Examples that come to mind are telephone or energy charges, which consist of a fixed charge plus a variable consumption charge. Other, less visible costs may be semi-fixed (or semi-variable) in nature and need to be split into their two components before the data can be used.

It is probably true that break-even charts are seen more often in textbooks than in real life. This is partly due to their limitations regarding linearity of costs, and in the case of multi-product firms a change in the product mix will invalidate the sales and costs lines. No break-even chart can predict the sales level at any given price—only market research can attempt that feat!

Nevertheless, the concept of break-even is very important for managers to understand, even if they do not go as far as constructing and using the charts. The underlying principle that a certain level of activity is needed to recover fixed overheads is crucial to survival. Put another way, there are limits to the fixed overheads a firm can afford!

CONTRIBUTION ANALYSIS

The term 'contribution' has a special meaning in accounting and can be said to be the difference between the sales value and the variable costs. This definition applies equally to one unit as to a product line or service. Contribution is therefore a kind of profit before all the fixed costs are taken into account, and probably lies somewhere between gross profit and net profit in most organizations.

Contribution = sales value – variable costs

There are a number of uses of contribution, one of which provides an explanation of why organizations sometimes charge less than normal prices (based on full cost), and why firms sometimes run special promotions from time to time when orders are low.

Special pricing

Take a firm with three product lines, A, B and C. With the contribution approach, common fixed costs are not apportioned to individual products but left as a total sum to which each product contributes. This has the advantage that when the volume of any product line is varied, by definition only the sales revenue and the variable costs will change proportionately. The fixed costs will remain unaltered in total. Sample figures are used in Figure 8.6 to illustrate this approach.

	Product			
	A	B	C	Total
	£000	£000	£000	£000
Sales	160	360	280	800
Less: Variable costs	120	180	128	428
Contribution	40	180	152	372
Less: Common fixed costs				320
Profit				52

Figure 8.6 *Contribution analysis by product*

We now want to see how analysing the cost information in this way helps managers to reach decisions about pricing a special order.

Example

A new export customer has offered to buy 30 per cent more of Product B, but only at 90 per cent of the normal price. The firm has spare capacity to cope with such an order without detriment to existing customers. Other orders are thought to be unlikely in the near future when this order would be processed. If the new order is accepted the variable costs will increase pro rata, but an additional shipping cost of £3000 will be incurred. The new situation is shown in Figure 8.7 when an increased contribution of £40,200 is earned, increasing profits by this same amount as no additional fixed costs were incurred.

	Product				
		Old	Extra		
	A	B	B	C	Total
	£000	£000	£000	£000	£000
Sales	160	360	97.2	280	897.2
Less: Variable costs	120	180	57.0	128	485.0
Contribution	40	180	40.2	152	412.2
Less: Common fixed costs					320.0
Profit					92.2

Figure 8.7 *Result of additional order at special price*

Some caveats must be mentioned here before you go rushing out to take on work, or sell, at less than full cost. If all work had been costed on this basis, the firm may not be making any profit at all! Also, the firm would not want to use its spare capacity in this way if it was able to get enough customers to pay normal prices. Nor would it want this customer to be in competition with its existing export customers. Selling at below full cost prices has to be seen as a temporary measure which allows a firm to make more profit, or a smaller loss, than it would otherwise do at that particular time.

Specific fixed costs

The above approach of putting all fixed costs into one pot may not be very realistic. It is likely that some fixed overheads, for example management staff or use of equipment, may be specific to one product line only. This information is relevant, say, if the firm was considering closing down a particular line. In this case the specific fixed costs relating just to that line would be saved in addition to its variable costs. If the total of all costs saved exceeds the sales revenue of that line then it is beneficial to close it down. Figure 8.8 illustrates this approach, now assuming that of the £320,000 fixed costs shown in Figure 8.6, some £50,000, £40,000 and £60,000 respectively are specific to the three lines A, B and C.

	Product			
	A	B	C	Total
	£000	£000	£000	£000
Sales	160	360	280	800
Less: Variable costs	120	180	128	428
Contribution	40	180	152	372
Less: Specific fixed costs	50	40	60	150
Net contribution	(10)	140	92	222
Less: Common fixed costs				170
Profit				52

Figure 8.8 *Effect of specific fixed costs*

When costs are analysed in this way, you can see that Product A is not worthwhile as it does not recover its own specific fixed costs, let alone make any contribution to common fixed costs and profit. However, in practice there may be marketing or operational reasons why a product line (A) may not be closed without affecting demand for other product lines (B or C).

Contribution ratio

Another use of the concept of contribution is in measuring product profitability. Instead of using either gross or net profit margins to do this, a contribution ratio can be calculated. This expresses the contribution as a percentage of the sales price. Again using the original data in Figure 8.6 to illustrate, the contribution ratios for each of the product lines is now shown in Figure 8.9.

	Product			
	A	B	C	Total
	£000	£000	£000	£000
Sales	160	360	280	800
Less: Variable costs	120	180	128	428
Contribution	40	180	152	372
Contribution ratio	25%	50%	54%	46%

Figure 8.9 *Contribution ratios*

Product managers and sales representatives may argue about the profit margins on their products because of the perceived, or actual, unfairness of fixed overhead apportionments to their products. It is much harder to argue against contribution ratios as a measure of product performance.

As the use of activity-based costing increases, resulting in more accurate and believable total product costs, these arguments about the fairness of overhead charges to individual product lines should diminish.

Another use of the contribution ratio is in the setting of selling prices. If the existing fixed overheads are added to the desired level of profit, this gives the total contribution needed to be earned from all product sales. If this required total contribution is now expressed as a percentage of the forecast total sales, this gives the average contribution ratio required on all sales. Selling prices of individual products can now be checked or preset against this contribution ratio criterion, to the extent that prices are cost-based.

Unit contribution

Another useful idea is that of unit contribution, which you can use to calculate the break-even point, or the volume required to achieve a certain level of profit.

Example

M Ltd is considering a reduction of 10 per cent in the price of one of their products in an attempt to boost sales volume and market share. The directors want to know what increase in sales volume is needed after the price reduction to make the same profit of £240,000 as before. The sales price and variable cost per unit are £200 and £120 respectively, and total fixed costs are £80,000.

Total contribution required = fixed costs + profit = £320,000

Contribution per unit = selling price − variable cost per unit = £80

Required volume = £320,000/£80 = 4000 units

DIFFERENTIAL COSTING

For certain decisions it can be useful to show information for two alternative situations side by side, and to look at the overall difference between their total costs (or profit). This technique is often termed differential costing because we are looking at the differences in costs/revenue between the alternatives. If we apply this idea to an earlier example of choosing between taking a train or travelling by car to Edinburgh, we get the following:

	By rail	*By car*	*Difference*
	£	£	£
Local travel	2.00	nil	+2.00
Train fare	25.00	nil	+25.00
Car travel (variable costs)	nil	16.40	− 16.40
Car parking fee	nil	3.00	− 3.00
	27.00	19.40	+7.60

Make or buy

The idea of comparing differences in costs between alternatives also finds an application in *make or buy* situations. This does not just refer to physical products and the decision to buy in compared to making in-house, it can also be applied to any service activity, for example:

- employing own solicitors or engaging a professional firm;
- employing own catering staff or franchising out;
- employing own cleaners or putting out to contract.

Example

Assume an organization's office cleaning is contracted out at present, for a fee of £12,500. Alternatively the organization could employ its own part-time cleaners at a cost of £9,000 excluding employer's National Insurance contributions. Cover for sickness and holidays adds another 10 per cent to this figure. In either case the organization pays for the permanent hire of equipment at £80 per month and would have to buy cleaning materials costing £500 if it did its own cleaning.

Set out in a differential cost analysis, the picture looks like this:

	Own £	Contract £	Difference £
Cleaning materials	500	nil	− 500
Contract fee	nil	12,500	+12,500
Cleaners' wages	9,000	nil	− 9,000
Cover for sickness/holidays	900	nil	− 900
Hire of equipment	960	960	nil
Totals	11,360	13,460	+2,100

Our conclusion from this differential cost analysis is that the organization should employ its own cleaners because the contract cleaning has an additional annual cost of £2100.

Outsourcing

Another make or buy decision is found in the increasing trend to *outsourcing*. When applied to manufactured items, the decision to outsource is of strategic importance, particularly if it is made before any investment commences. The advantages of using a contract manufacturer for components or finished products include:

- reduced fixed asset and working capital requirements;
- no set-up, development and training costs;
- risk avoidance in uncertain markets;
- assured quality if suppliers are certified to BS5750;
- management can concentrate more on marketing and strategic issues.

These advantages may also have a downside. A company's ability to innovate and develop its product range may be weakened by outsourcing where the necessary know-how is retained by the contract manufacturers. If so, a company's existing competitive edge will diminish. You will find more information in articles by Johnson and Johnson[1] and Allen.[2]

SUMMARY

You have now been exposed to many different ways of looking at costs. This chapter on marginal costing uses cost information with a view to making short-term decisions, either to make more profit or to save existing costs.

These decisions are based on the behaviour of costs in certain situations when the level of activity changes. Some confusion exists between the identification of costs as either fixed or variable and what at first glance may seem a similar classification of costs as indirect or direct respectively. We hope you can now recognize the differences!

If you want to take this topic further, try reading the appropriate chapters of Drury's book on management and cost accounting listed in the Bibliography.

References

1. Johnson, D and Johnson, N (1991) 'Using contract manufacturers during a recession', *Management Accounting* (UK), June.
2. Allen, D (1993) 'International sourcing', *Management Accounting* (UK), October.

9

Budgetary control

Two of the key roles performed by you and other managers are those of planning and control. In a financial context, plans are often referred to as *budgets,* and control as *budgetary control.* By preparing financial plans for each financial responsibility centre, and monitoring actual performance against them on a regular monthly basis, top management ensure they get no nasty surprises at the end of the financial year when the annual accounts are produced.

There are a number of levels of financial responsibility centres, starting at the lowest level of *cost centre,* rising through *revenue centres* and *profit centres* to *investment centres* at the top of the pyramid. Sitting on top is the parent company or parent group of companies and the revenue budget for the total entity is the amalgamation of all the budgets below. The revenue budget is in effect the budgeted profit and loss account for the company or the group. Consolidation of the responsibility centres

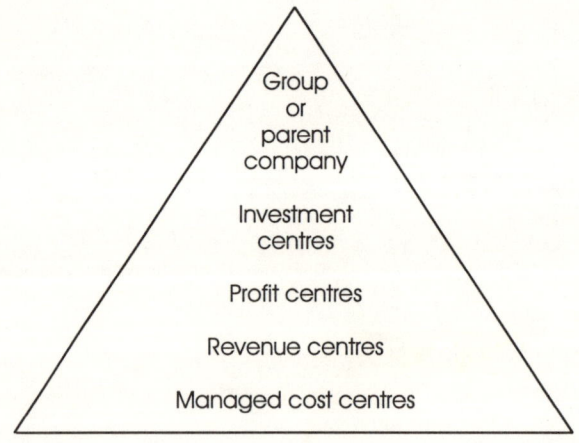

Figure 9.1 *Pyramid of financial responsibility centres*

beneath any one level is also possible. This tiered approach to budget planning and monitoring is shown in Figure 9.1.

We can think of budgetary control, as we did product cost control, as a continuous cycle of events, consisting of four main stages as illustrated in Figure 9.2. This starts with the setting of budgets for costs and revenues in the financial responsibility centres; next comes the measuring of actual costs and revenues as each month passes; then a comparison of actuals with budget which will throw up variances; action will now be needed to correct adverse variances and build on any favourable variances; finally, a new budget or forecast is prepared, so completing the cycle.

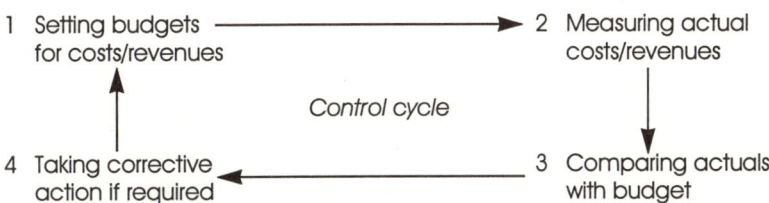

Figure 9.2 *Budgetary control cycle*

Budgets and budgetary control are applicable to all organizations, both profit seeking and non-profit seeking, in both manufacturing and service industries. Any differences between them are reflected in their different financial objectives and different functional departments or activities. Puxty and Lyall[1] found in their survey of over 400 UK companies that 94 per cent of respondents used budgeting systems, a level backed-up by a more recent survey of UK manufacturing companies by Drury et al.[2]

Most large organizations have corporate and strategic plans that are concerned with long-term plans to meet broad objectives, typically over the next five years. Budgets are an expression of those financial plans to meet objectives in the coming accounting year, but must also be compatible with the longer-term objectives.

Short-term financial objectives in profit-seeking organizations might be to:

■ capture a certain percentage share of the market;
■ earn a stated amount of profit;
■ achieve a specified return on the capital employed in the business.

In non-profit-seeking organizations the financial objective may simply be not to overspend, namely, to keep within a grant or budget allocation provided for that activity. This will also be a key objective of individual cost centres within a profit-seeking organization.

By using a system of budgetary control, top management can:

- delegate day-to-day responsibility to lower levels of management;
- coordinate the various activities to achieve common goals;
- retain overall control;
- manage by exception;
- have ready-made yardsticks to monitor managers' performance.

When properly implemented, budgets act as a motivating tool. You may know from your own experience that the way systems are introduced and operated can either harness co-operation or encourage individuals to beat the system. We return to these behavioural aspects later in the chapter.

REVENUE BUDGETING SYSTEMS

Revenue budgets are concerned with planned revenue and operating costs going into the profit and loss account or other similar statements. When preparing revenue budgets, there are a number of different approaches. These include:

- 'bottom-up' budgeting;
- 'top-down' budgeting;
- incremental budgeting;
- zero based budgeting;
- priority based budgeting;
- fixed budgeting;
- flexible budgeting.

Bottom-up/top-down budgeting

Neither bottom-up nor top-down budgeting is a budgeting system in itself. They are different philosophies on where to start the budgeting process. A *bottom-up* approach is when the lowest level of financial responsibility centres prepare their own budgets and feed them up to the next level, for example when cost centres feed up to the profit centre above them. These budgets pass through successive levels until they are amalgamated into the overall parent or group budgeted profit and loss account. Depending on the results portrayed, alterations can be requested by top management to enable their broad financial objectives to be achieved.

Conversely, a top-down approach applies when the profit centre imposes cost budgets or sales budgets on the cost or revenue centres beneath it. In this case, both ownership of the budgets and the motivation to achieve them will be diminished.

Incremental budgeting

As the term incremental budgeting suggests, it means taking last year's budget and adjusting it for changes in costs, prices and activity levels. The easy option is to add the rate of inflation to each cost heading and make that the new budget. A major drawback with this approach is that it does not lead to questioning of existing practices and inefficiencies. There is no constructive challenging of the status quo.

Zero based budgeting (ZBB)

The zero based budgeting approach starts with a clean sheet and builds up budgets from scratch. In this way managers have to justify resource requirements expressed as costs in their budgets. Each item of expenditure is questioned: first as to whether it should exist at all, and only then as to its precise level. ZBB also questions whether there is a better way of working and organizing that would result in lower costs.

This philosophy may be applied throughout the organization or restricted to administrative functions where it is particularly relevant in questioning redundant clerical procedures. A major criticism of ZBB is the time and effort needed, when compared to the quicker incremental budgeting approach. A compromise solution is sometimes adopted of working on incremental budgeting most years, with ZBB every few years as a check on inefficiencies that may have crept in. ZBB could thus rotate round different departments each year, so keeping the work effort and disruption in check.

Some writers incorporate *priority based budgeting* (PBB) into ZBB. In a system of PBB, managers identify the activities in their responsibility centres and package them into separate *decision packages*. According to Connolly and Ashworth,[3] a decision package contains the following:

- a cost, in terms of both human resource and money;
- a description of what activities will be undertaken with the resource;
- a statement of the benefits that will ensue if the activity is funded in the budget;
- a statement of the consequences that will occur if the resource is denied.

All decision packages from all managers are then combined into one list and meetings held to rank them in order of priority. Top management then have to decide how far up the list to go with the resources that can be made available. Decision packages above the cut-off point are denied any resource and are therefore redundant.

ZBB is also appropriate to the new thinking on 'business process re-engineering' (BPR). Hammer[4] made the term re-engineering known to a wider audience and his book, co-authored with Champy on *Re-engineering the corporation* (see Bibliography) is responsible for the current interest in BPR.

In the past, companies have tended to organize on functional lines with tight departmental boundaries. A business process is a series of interrrelated activities that transcends departmental boundaries in the delivery of an output, somewhat akin to an activity in ABC thinking. The launch of a new product or service is a good example.

BPR proponents argue that a company should structure itself around business processes geared to delivering the company's products and services to the customer[5]. This is not a one-off exercise but part of the search for *continuous improvement*.

The benefits of BPR include:

■ delayering the vertical hierarchies inherent in departmental organizations;
■ use of IT to handle cross-functional activities and speed up throughput;
■ increased focus on the customer.

Incremental budgets based on functional departments are totally inappropriate for this new way of thinking. ZBB incorporating activity based budgeting is much more in tune with the ongoing search for continuous improvement through change. Connolly and Ashworth's article on 'An integrated activity-based approach to budgeting'[3] is recommended for its lucid treatment of activity- and priority-based budgeting.

Fixed budgeting

The word 'fixed' denotes that a budget is prepared for levels of activity determined at the outset and left unchanged thereafter. The consequence of this is that any variance resulting from a comparison of an actual cost with a budgeted cost can be misleading. This is because the actual cost is being compared with a budgeted cost for a level of activity that did not materialize. This can be overcome by the use of a 'flexible budgeting' system.

Flexible budgeting

Flexible budgeting entails the preparation of not just one but a series of budgets for varying levels of activity. The purpose is to allow the comparison of the actual costs incurred with the flexed budget that corresponds to the level of activity actually achieved, instead of comparing actual costs with a fixed budget for an activity level that never happened!

The following example illustrates the difference between fixed and flexible budgeting, when a misleading favourable variance of £250 is reported on a fixed budgeting system, while flexible budgeting correctly reports an adverse variance of £150.

Example

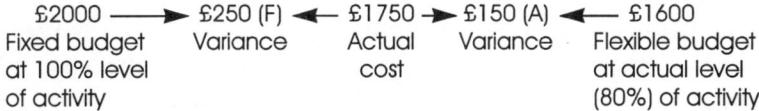

£2000 ⟶	£250 (F) ⟵	£1750 ⟶	£150 (A) ⟵	£1600
Fixed budget at 100% level of activity	Variance	Actual cost	Variance	Flexible budget at actual level (80%) of activity

The survey by Drury et al[2] of UK manufacturing organizations found that only 42 per cent of all respondents declared their use of flexible budgets. However, when analysed by size of organization, over half of the larger, but only 22 per cent of the smaller organizations used flexible budgeting.

PREPARATION OF BUDGETS

The accounting year is the natural period for the preparation of budgets. The year is then broken down into shorter periods, often of about one month's duration, although retail organizations may go for weekly periods. Your own organization may use one of the following short intervals for *phasing* budgets and as intervals for their subsequent control:

- one week;
- four weeks;
- a calendar month;
- a specified number of working days.

Medium-sized and larger organizations will issue a set of budget instructions prior to budget preparation, usually about 3—4 months before the end of the current financial year. This will contain details of requirements regarding:

- broad objectives;
- relevant parameters;
- coordination requirements;
- budget timetable;
- treatment of inflation;
- phasing of costs/revenues over periods;
- incremental or zero based approach.

Consideration has to be given whether to appoint a budget officer, charged with the responsibility of co-ordinating the whole budget effort and linking the various functions, or to form a budgeting committee. This may comprise representatives of top management, finance directors and functional managers. Its role is to issue guidelines to all budget holders and help with co-ordination across functions so that all parties are working on compatible plans.

When they have finally been accepted by the budget committee, the functional budgets are aggregated into a master budget, consisting of a budgeted income statement (broken down into short periods) and a projected balance sheet at the year-end. If approved by the board, this becomes the policy to be pursued in the coming year.

In many organizations this procedure, outlined in Figure 9.3, is assisted by an accountant or budget officer, who provides information and advice to all the parties concerned.

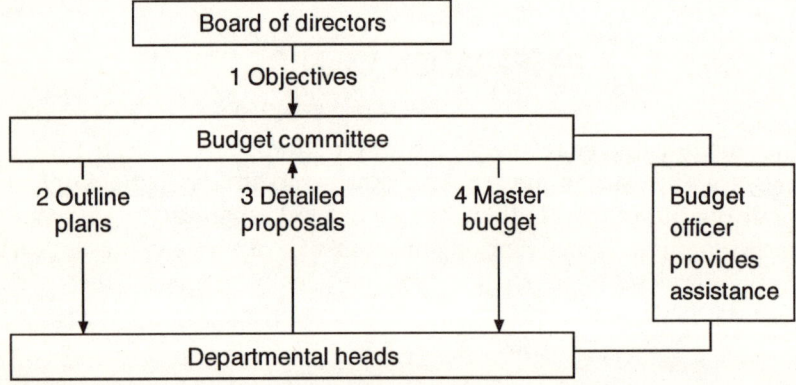

Figure 9.3 *Budget preparation*

The key or limiting factor needs to be identified before budgeting can start. The key factor in budgeting is whatever limits or restricts the growth of an organization at this point. You might recognize one of the following as the key factor in your own organization:

- sales demand;
- capacity;
- skilled employees;
- equipment;
- working capital (including cash) requirements;
- physical space.

Assuming sales is the key factor for a company, this places the major responsibility for budgeting on the shoulders of the sales manager or sales director. The sales team will have to consider the present level of trading, anticipate future trading conditions and use feedback from their sales force or market research reports to prepare a sales budget.

The survey by Drury et al[2] found that 85 per cent of respondent organizations often or always used subjective estimates based on experience to forecast budgeted sales revenue. Statistical forecasting and market research were also used by 31 per cent and 36 per cent respectively, implying the use of multiple methods in some cases.

A sales budget is not a single sales figure for the year but a detailed breakdown of sales:

- by type;
- by customer;
- by region; and
- by month.

Once sales have been specified, the production or operations budget comes next, depending on whether the organization is a manufacturer or not. This takes the sales requirements and allows for changes in stock levels, the use of subcontractors, lead times, and other factors, so that the operational requirements will result. The *production or operations budget* specifies:

- the volume of output;
- when it is needed;
- which departments will produce it; and
- the cost of the labour, materials and other resources to be consumed.

These two sales and operations budgets determine the level of activity for the whole organization and the level of service activity required from the marketing, sales administration, distribution and other administration departments, like accounting and personnel, who need to construct their own overhead budgets. This budgeting process is illustrated in Figure 9.4, although it must be said that functional structures can vary widely between organizations and may be activity based in some.

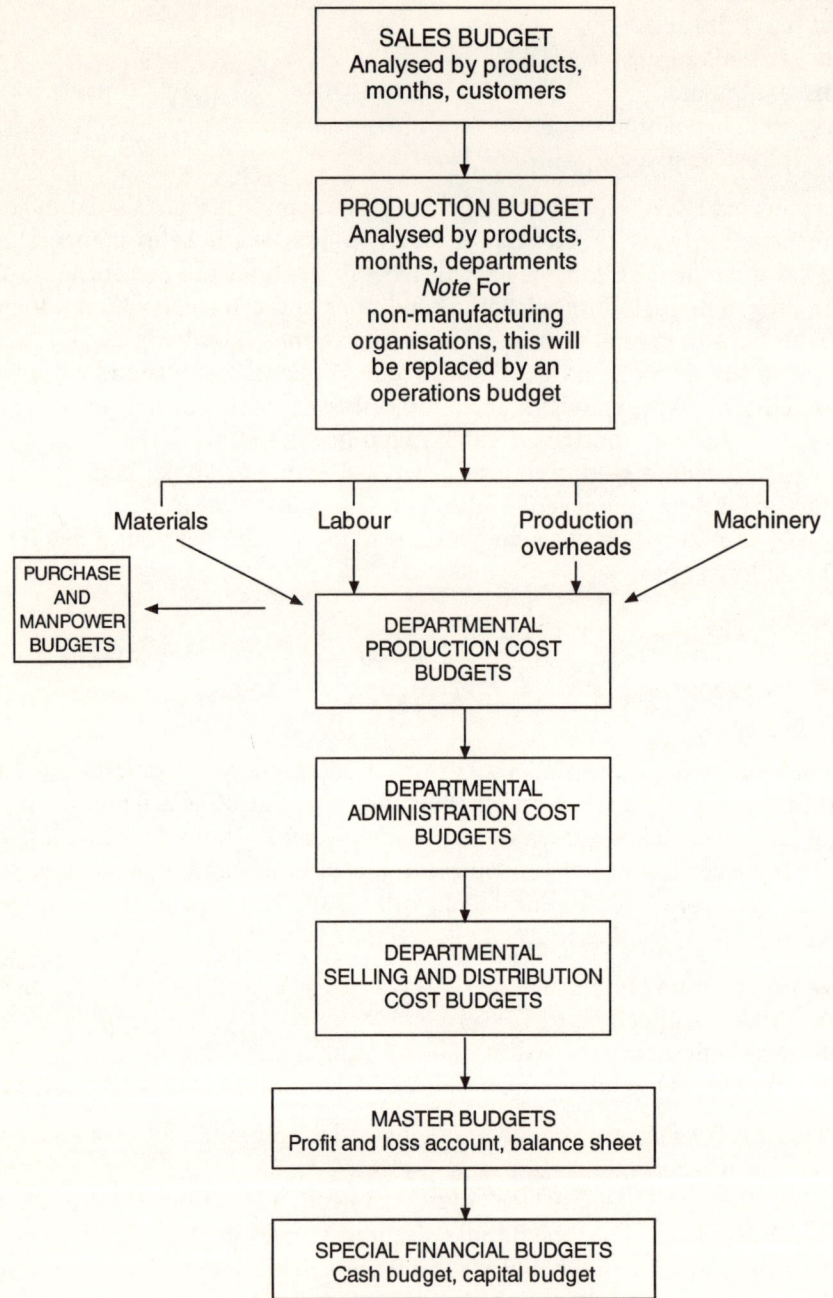

Figure 9.4 *The budgeting process*

Departmental overhead budgets are then prepared. The production department overheads are geared to the production levels specified for those departments. Similarly, the selling and distribution overhead costs will be geared to the sales budget quantities. Other administrative departments' budgets will be determined by the overall level of activity.

Research and development will also have a budget, but this is more a long-term investment of funds not closely related to short-term needs nor to the other functional budgets. However, research activity is usually charged against income as and when it is incurred, so it has a place in the revenue budget. Control over research spending is exercised by monitoring the overall spending, but this is augmented by specific control over individual projects against any milestones reached. This is somewhat similar to the way that control is exercised over capital projects, as discussed later.

In this way the various functional and departmental budgets are prepared which facilitate the composition of subordinate budgets for material purchases and human resource planning. The functional budgets form the basis for a *master budget* which includes a budgeted income statement and a projected balance sheet. It is this master budget which goes to the board for approval, along with a budgeted cash flow statement and a capital expenditure budget.

MANAGING THE BUDGET

The comparison of actual results with budget can take place at two levels. Each department manager is fed information about the costs under his or her control, comparing actual costs against budget for the month under review with a further comparison for the number of months of the budget year so far expired. An example of this is given in Figure 9.5, where you will see a distinction being made between controllable and non-controllable expenditure. This allows the manager concerned to monitor progress against budget above the line for items over which he or she has both responsibility and authority. Other overheads and head office charges can then be shown below the line as non-controllables to allow the fuller picture of responsibility without authority to be seen.

At a higher level in the organization—at executive level and possibly at board meetings—the budgeted profit and loss account is compared with the actual results achieved month by month. Very small organizations may also use this global approach in place of departmental budget reports since their size inhibits a breakdown into functional departments.

Month..Dept..							
Cost code	Description	Current month			Cumulative		
		Budget	Actual	Variance	Budget	Actual	Variance
320	Controllable Salaries etc.	£ 3,600	£ 3,400	£ 200 F	£ 23,000	£ 24,300	£ 1,300 A
710	Non-controllable HO charges etc.	1,000	1,100	100 A	7,000	7,700	700 A

Figure 9.5 *Monthly budget report*

Software is available, or specific programmes can be written, to produce monthly reports for each department which integrate with the total financial results. Much budgeting work can now be performed on standard spreadsheets such as Excel or Lotus 1-2-3 without having to go to additional expense.

Variances

You will see that the variances disclosed in Figure 9.5 are the difference between the actual cost and the budgeted cost for each cost heading. Managers may be required to explain any significant variances each month, being ones that exceed a certain sum of money or ones that exceed a certain percentage variation. In this way, valuable time and effort are not wasted investigating trivial differences.

Not only are explanations required from a manager but action too! An overspend in one month is not necessarily critical if the cumulative position is satisfactory. The opposite is the case in Figure 9.5, where the one month's salaries are within budget but the cumulative position is well overspent. This may be due to excessive overtime which has recently been curtailed as a result of a previous month's cumulative adverse variance.

Excessive spending will need to be cut back unless there is an imperative reason for it. Sometimes an overspend on one budget heading can be alleviated by transferring some unused budget allocation to the overspent heading. This process is known as 'virement' but not all organizations allow it.

Possible actions you can consider to cut back on excessive spending include:

■ reduce staffing;
■ cut back on overtime;
■ switch to part-time staff in slack periods;
■ check material wastage levels;
■ find cheaper sources of supply;

- monitor energy efficiency;
- conduct essential training only.

BEHAVIOURAL ASPECTS

The way in which budgeting is implemented and managed within an organization can give rise to a number of behavioural consequences, some of which are favourable but others can have an adverse effect. Likely situations are:

- top-down imposed budgets;
- accountant-run budget systems;
- padded budgets;
- late budget reports;
- non-controllable expenditure.

Imposed budgets

If you are handed a budget and told to get on with it, you are less likely to feel ownership towards that budget than if you had taken part in its construction and the reasoned arguments leading to the budget allocation on each cost heading.

Bottom-up budgets bring ownership and motivation to achieve targets, even when the original budget submission is tightened as part of the overall co-ordination and the need for a viable outcome for the total organization.

Accountant-run budgeting systems

Budgeting needs the involvement and backing of the chief executive and board if it is to be successful. It is a management tool that happens to use financial information. The board should approve the yearly budget and be seen to monitor its progress at monthly intervals.

The active involvement of most senior management, with their experience of the key functional activities, is essential if realistic, but challenging, budgets are to be prepared. No matter how good financial people are in an organization, they can not realistically be expected to be skilful in sales, operations and other activities.

Padded budgets

A bottom-up approach to budgeting could lead to managers 'padding' their budget because experience has shown they can get away with it, or they have always observed that a particular percentage cut is applied each year. If successful, a padded budget should show up in a consistent underspend each year, but this consequence should attract future scrutiny of that manager's budget proposals.

Budgets should be set at realistic levels with neither padding nor *budget slack* built in. On the other hand, they should not be set too optimistically such that they mislead top management on the revenue or expenditure levels that can realistically be achieved.

Late reporting

If you are requested to explain budget variances on a monthly report that is issued, say, three weeks after the end of the period being reported on, you would be hard put to remember precisely what had been going on the previous month. This difficulty leads to frustration and inefficiency all round and should be avoided at all costs, otherwise the budgeting system falls into disrepute.

There should be no excuse for delays in recording in-house labour and material costs. A frequent excuse offered for the delay in recording other expenses is that an invoice has not yet been received from the supplier. It is not too difficult in this age of information technology to use accruals for all invoices not received within a few days of the month-end, so allowing the production of timely budget reports.

Non-controllable expenditure

There are arguments for showing all expenditure relating to a responsibility centre on a budget report comparing actual costs with budgeted costs. This allows a full view of the performance of that centre to be obtained. The difficulty arises with expenditure which is rightly included, but over which the manager of the centre has no authority. Charges for notional rent, apportionments of business rates, group service levies and headquarters overhead charges could be examples.

The answer is to split the budget report into two sections under the following headings:

■ controllable items;
■ non-controllable items.

In this way both points of view are catered for. The manager is held responsible for the controllable costs only, but sight is not lost of the cost of all the resources consumed by that responsibility centre.

The survey of UK manufacturing organizations by Drury et al[2] found that 23 per cent of respondents included controllable costs only in performance reports to budget holders. Three-quarters of the respondents presented information on both controllable and non-controllable costs, of which 52 per cent distinguished between them but 23 per cent did not.

CAPITAL BUDGETING

Before individual projects are selected, top management need to decide how much capital to make available in the coming budget year. This is mainly determined by:

- ongoing projects previously authorized;
- the amount of assets that need replacing;
- the opportunities for new investment;
- the current size of the gearing ratio;
- whether market conditions allow a rights issue.

When compiling the total capital budget for the coming year, firms need to categorize investments and then prioritize those categories. A sample picture might emerge as:

1. Continued spending on previous years' projects not yet completed.
2. Legal, safety or environmental requirements.
3. Replacement of worn-out assets.
4. Cost-saving investments.
5. New product investment.
6. Diversification investment.

Individual projects need to go through a screening process. First, the purpose of the investment needs to accord with organizational objectives. Then a cost-benefit analysis (the subject of the next chapter) needs to be carried out to ensure financial viability so far as is possible when forecasting future events. Finally, any non-quantifiable costs and benefits need to be considered, along with the track record of the management team, before authorization is granted.

Once a project has been authorized it needs careful monitoring in just the same way as a revenue budget for a cost centre. The difference is that in capital budgeting the focus is on the project itself, irrespective of which cost centres have contributed to its cost. The project manager needs feedback on the total spending to date, broken down in some detail, related to the amount budgeted in the financial year and authorized over the project's life. This manager will also be required to make new forecasts of the *cost to completion* at regular monthly or quarterly intervals.

Top management will require feedback on the state of capital spending, and a suitable format is shown in Figure 9.6. This discloses that the second project is on target, the third project will be slightly underspent, but the first project is likely to be £24,000 (7 per cent) overspent by the time it is completed.

Capital budget report

Actual/projected expenditure

Project title	Project number	Previous years	Current year	Total to date	Projected to complete	Authorized amount	Variance
		£	£	£	£	£	£
Teesside	37649	216580	58400	274980	49000	300000	23980A
Filters	37650	—	26900	26900	13100	40000	nil
Car park	37651	12000	5500	17500	nil	18000	500F
Totals			90800	319380	62100	358000	23480A

Figure 9.6 *Capital budget report for top management*

SUMMARY

You may find it useful to obtain a copy of the revenue budget report for your department or unit. Study the format and information given in the light of the above discussion, and judge the report's suitability for the purpose of allowing you or another manager to measure, monitor and control the cost of resources consumed in your unit. If you are likely to be involved with capital expenditure proposals, study the authorization and monitoring system employed by your organization.

If you want to take budgeting further—and this is a key area for managers to master if they are to be on top of their job—try reading the appropriate chapters of Drury's book listed in the Bibliography, and follow up the references given in this chapter.

References

1. Puxty, A G and Lyall, D (1989) *Cost control into the 1990s*, CIMA.

2. Drury, C, Braund, S, Osborne, P and Tayles, M (1993) *A survey of management accounting practices in UK manufacturing companies*, ACCA.

3. Connolly, T and Ashworth, G (1994) 'An integrated activity-based approach to budgeting', *Management Accounting* (UK), March.

4. Hammer, M (1990) 'Re-engineering work: don't automate, obliterate', *Harvard Business Review*, July/August.

5. Classe, A (1993) 'Don't tinker with it: BPR it!', *Accountancy*, July.

10

Capital investment appraisal

An alternative title for this chapter could be 'cost-benefit analysis'. When applied to the investment of capital this sums up exactly what appraisal is all about, namely the weighing up of costs against benefits to measure overall viability. Any capital project whose benefits do not recoup all its costs over its expected life is financially unacceptable, unless there are other non-monetary benefits to take into account. Not only should a project recoup all its capital and running costs over its life, it must also earn a surplus with which to reward the providers of the capital—shareholders and financial institutions in particular.

The term *cost-benefit analysis* also has a more specific meaning in the public sector. It refers to the weighing up of the costs and benefits of all the parties affected by the investment under review, not just those of the investing organization. True cost-benefit analyses include measurements of costs and benefits relating to employment, health, leisure and environmental effects. Economists have to find ways to put monetary values on these social costs and benefits.

If you work in a public service, investment appraisal is as applicable as it is to any other manager in the private sector. For example, investments in information technology are equally relevant to public and private sectors, and are an important source of cost savings.

TYPES OF INVESTMENT SITUATION

You may recognize some of the following investment situations where an appraisal takes place:

- *Expansion*—assessing the viability of expanding existing product lines requiring new investment in buildings, plant and working capital.

- *Cost saving*—for example the investment in new technology has to be justified by savings or a greater output.
- *Replacement*—deciding whether and when to replace an old machine with a new one to save operating costs and increase quality.
- *Alternative choice*—deciding between alternative investments to achieve the same ends where their ratios of capital to running costs differ.
- *Financing*—comparing the cost of purchasing an asset outright with the alternative cost of leasing.

All these situations require that capital to be spent initially, with the aim that it is recouped from the savings or profits that result from the project. This capital has a cost which is taken into account by the discounted cash flow technique which is discussed below.

COST OF CAPITAL

In the public sector borrowing is the sole source of capital. Private sector organizations have two main sources: companies either borrow capital from financial institutions or they obtain capital from their shareholders. The latter can be done either by selling more shares or by retaining some of the profit each year and not paying it all out as dividends. UK companies, in particular, rely heavily on retained profits as a major source of additional capital.

In the context of investment appraisal, we are interested in the cost of *new* capital rather than *old* capital, as it is new capital which will be invested in new projects. An organization which borrowed money many years ago at, say, 5 per cent should not regard this as its current cost of capital if new investments are to be financed by capital costing, say, 10 per cent.

Cost of public sector capital

Any public sector organization which totally funds itself by borrowed capital, or government borrowing on its behalf, has no problem in determining its cost of capital. This equates to the current interest rate needed to sell long-dated and relatively low-risk government stocks at par.

At the time of writing, this long-dated rate of interest is approximately 8 per cent. This should be regarded as the minimum required on any new investment in this sector when the project cash flows are expressed in *nominal* terms.

Real and nominal cost of capital

Assume 8 per cent is the current long-term borrowing rate. This is the *nominal cost of debt capital*; the word nominal implies that it is expressed in money terms, including compensation for inflation. For example, if inflation is 3 per cent, then the *real cost of debt capital* is approximately 5 per cent (8 per cent– 3 per cent) in this example.

When you appraise a project you can do it in real terms by expressing all future costs and benefits at today's prices, or you can inflate the yearly costs and benefits to express them in nominal terms. Whichever way you express the yearly costs and benefits, you must use a cost of capital compatible with your treatment of inflation.

You can do this in one of the following two ways:

- expressing the yearly costs and benefits in real terms (all at today's prices) and using the *real cost of capital* in the discounting process;
- expressing the yearly costs and benefits in nominal terms (all at inflated prices) each year and using the *nominal cost of capital* for discounting.

Cost of private sector debt capital

In the case of a company, the cost of debt is the rate of interest which has to be paid on new loans to get them taken up by investors at par. Such rates vary over time, with the size of the loan and with the degree of risk attached to each company. It is for these reasons that the cost of debt for a company, ignoring tax considerations, is greater than the cost of debt for the government.

All companies are allowed to charge interest payments as an expense in their profit and loss account before tax is computed on any profits. This *tax shield* reduces the effective rate of interest paid by companies in a somewhat similar manner to tax relief on mortgage interest for individuals. The difference is that there is no upper limit on the amount of tax relief for companies! If a company pays corporation tax at 33 per cent, then the cost of its debt carrying an interest rate of, say, 9 per cent, reduces to 6 per cent after the tax shield is deducted.

Cost of private companies' share capital

The reward to shareholders is a little more complicated than assuming it is just the cost of dividends paid. Basically, the cost of equity capital is the return investors require the company to earn on all shareholders' funds invested in the business. This may be measured directly in a private company by asking its few shareholders individually what return they require.

However, it may also be measured indirectly by the *dividend growth model*. This approach calculates the dividend yield and adds the dividend growth rate expected of the company, possibly based on past experience and adjusted for future prospects. Because of tax relief on interest payments, and an increased level of risk for shareholders, we would expect the cost of equity to be more than the cost of borrowed funds.

The model takes the expected dividend for the coming year and expresses it as a percentage of the current share price to obtain the *dividend yield*. To this is added the expected growth rate in dividends in the coming years. The current share price can either be based on recent transactions between investors in that company, or based on a price/earnings approach for recent sales of shares in similar companies.

Cost of equity = dividend yield + dividend growth rate

In terms of a formula, the dividend growth model looks like this:

$$Ke = \frac{Di}{Po}\% + g\%$$

Where: Ke = cost of equity
Di = next year's dividend
Po = market price of share
g = growth rate of annual dividends

Example

Graham Ltd currently pays a net dividend of 10p on each ordinary share, some of which recently changed hands between private investors at £2 each. Growth of profits and dividends in recent years has averaged 10 per cent, and this process is expected to continue. The cost of equity (Ke) using the dividend growth formula is therefore:

$$Ke = \frac{Di}{Po}\% + g\% = \frac{10p}{£2}\% + 10\% = 15\%$$

The weighted average cost of capital (WACC)

Having identified the cost of debt and the cost of equity for a private company, the overall cost of its capital can now be found. This takes

Example

Assume your company tries to keep its capital structure in the ratio of 20 per cent borrowed capital to 80 per cent equity. The cost of new borrowing is 9 per cent, which reduces to 6 per cent after 33 per cent corporation tax relief. The cost of new equity is, say, 15 per cent for your company in nominal terms. The overall weighted average cost of capital for this company is just over 13 per cent, as calculated below:

Type of capital	Proportion	After-tax cost	Weighted cost
9% Borrowed capital	0.20	6.0%	1.2%
Equity	0.80	15.0%	12.0%
	1.00		13.2%

This weighted average cost is the nominal post-tax cost of capital. Part of this 13 per cent reward goes to compensate for the erosion of capital by inflation, and only the remainder is a real return. Taking the earlier example of inflation at 3 per cent, this would reduce the real cost of capital to about 10 per cent (13 per cent − 3 per cent) for this company.

the cost of each type of capital and averages them out after taking account of their respective proportions.

Quoted company cost of capital

The use of the weighted average cost of capital may not be restricted to private companies if research findings are any guide (see below). However, a modern approach to finding the cost of equity for a quoted company is based on the *capital asset pricing model* or CAPM for short. The idea behind this is to say that the return to an investor is in two parts. The first part equates to the return currently available on a risk-free investment, say in short-dated government stocks. The other part is a risk premium relating to the degree of market risk attaching to an investment in that particular company's shares, including the financial risk attached to the gearing in its capital structure.

The risk premium is based on the calculation of a 'beta' factor which measures the sensitivity of a particular company's share price to general stock market movements such as measured by the FT All-Share Index. A share with a beta of 1.0 is expected, on average, to move in line with the market. A share with a beta of 1.4 is predicted to move 1.4 per cent on average for a 1.0 per cent change by the market, while a share with a beta of 0.6 is expected to move 0.6 per cent on average for a 1.0 per cent move by the market. The LBS Risk Measurement Service calculates the betas of some 2000 UK companies quoted on the London Stock Exchange, with most betas lying within the range 0.5–1.5.

To express the cost of equity using the CAPM approach, the formula would be:

$Ke = Rf + B(Rm - Rf)$

Where: Ke = cost of equity

Example

Where Rf = 5 per cent, Rm = 13 per cent and B = 0.7, the cost of equity becomes:

Ke	=	Rf	+	B	$(Rm - Rf)$
10.6%	=	5%	+	0.7	(13% – 5%)

Rf = risk-free return
Rm = market portfolio return
B = beta factor

When appraising an individual project that is expected to have the same risk profile as the whole company, the cost of equity derived from the CAPM approach is appropriate as the required rate of return. Where the level of risk on a proposed project is not deemed to be the same as for the existing company, or where the level of gearing for the company changes significantly, then adjustments have to be made to the above formula to use it as the required rate of return on new projects. Discussion on these issues is outside the scope of this book but if you want to know more, try Drury's book listed in the Bibliography, or the explanatory articles provided by the London Business School Risk Measurement Service.

Although the CAPM approach might appear theoretically sound and an attractive way of allowing for risk in investment appraisal, the choice of appropriate betas for individual projects is not simple in practice. This might explain why researchers have found such a poor take-up of the idea in industry.

Pike and Ho[1] found that 84 per cent of their respondents never or rarely used beta analysis, while the study by Drury et al[2] of large manufacturing firms put the non-use as high as 97 per cent.

INCREMENTAL CASH FLOW MODEL

Every investment situation requires a forecast of its expected life and the monetary value of the yearly costs and benefits that will occur. These values are prepared on an incremental basis, meaning that only those costs and benefits which change as a direct result of making this investment are included. Furthermore, these costs and benefits are expressed in *cash flows*.

Sunk costs

Any development costs previously incurred are ignored, as would be the case with a market survey or the building of a prototype machine before any investment decision was made. These prior costs are known as *sunk costs* because the money has already been spent and this should not influence the later decision whether to invest or not. Inevitably, the greater the amount of sunk costs relative to the investment still to be made, the more likely the scheme will be to proceed because the benefits are related to a smaller investment.

Depreciation

When working out the incremental cash flows, depreciation is ignored as the whole of the cost of the investment is included at the time the investment is made. This is usually referred to as Year 0, being the first day of the first year in the life of the investment. If we included depreciation in the yearly costs, we would be guilty of double counting.

The other reason why depreciation is ignored is that these investment appraisal models are based on cash flows and *not* on the accounting concept of profit. Depreciation is not a cash flow! Cash inflows are given a positive sign and cash outflows a negative one in the model. These costs and benefits are set out with the years along

Example

A company is considering a cost saving investment of £10,000 that has annual running costs of £5000 and saves £8000 in each year of its five-year life.

Year	Capital cost £	Running costs £	Savings £	Net cash flow £
0	−10000			−10000
1		−5000	+8000	+3000
2		−5000	+8000	+3000
3		−5000	+8000	+3000
4		−5000	+8000	+3000
5		−5000	+8000	+3000
	−10,000	−25,000	+40,000	+5000

This investment has a surplus total net cash flow of £5000 at the end of its expected five-year life. This approach, however, has a serious weakness because the time value of money is ignored. For example, the saving of £8000 during year 1 is worth more than the saving of £8000 during year 2. The concept of the time value of money is discussed in more detail in the section on 'net present value'.

one axis and the items making up the cash flows along the other, as in the example below. The axes can be laid out either way round, and are often the reverse of those shown below in computer spreadsheet models.

Overhead costs

Some industries by their nature have numbers of large capital projects requiring the use of resources in their planning and supervision until completion. Take the case of a regional electricity company which has approved the construction of a new overhead line to distribute electricity. Engineers' time, office accommodation and travelling expenses will be incurred by the staff planning and supervising the construction of this line. Such overhead costs are a valid charge to the project and should be capitalized as such.

This has the effect of reducing the overhead charges appearing in the company profit and loss account by including such charges as a fixed asset cost in the balance sheet. This in no way invalidates the principle of preparing the cash flows on an incremental basis, even if a percentage oncost is used to transfer such costs from revenue expenditure to capital expenditure in the absence of a direct charging system.

APPRAISAL METHODS

There are a number of appraisal methods used to assess the worthwhileness of proposed investments. The main ones are:

■ payback period;
■ accounting rate of return;
■ net present value (NPV);
■ internal rate of return (IRR).

These appraisal methods are now examined in turn and the cash flow model above is used to demonstrate each one.

Payback period

The payback period method counts the number of years or months it takes for the cash inflows to recover the initial outlay. In the above example it takes over three years to recover the original investment of £10,000 at the rate of £3000 each year. More precisely, the payback period is three years and four months.

This payback criterion is not so easy to interpret, particularly when different investments may have different life expectancies. One way round this is to look at where payback lies relative to the expected life of the investment. In the above example, payback would not be completed until 67 per cent of the life was expired.

The survey by Drury et al[2] of UK manufacturing organizations found that payback was the most widely used appraisal technique, often used in conjunction with other techniques in larger organizations, but more often on its own in smaller companies. Drury also found that most respondents required a payback in 2–3 years and again a majority varied the payback period on individual projects when dealing with risk.

Accounting rate of return

In the accounting rate of return method the average profit per annum is expressed as a percentage of either the original investment or the average investment, being half the original amount as the investment depreciates from full cost down to zero over its expected life. In the above example the average profit is £1000 (£5000/5) after allowing for depreciation of the asset in full, which represents a 10 per cent return on the original investment of £10,000 or a 20 per cent return on the average investment of £5000 (£10,000/2).

The problem with using averages in the calculations is that they do not recognize the time value of money in each separate year, nor does the treatment of depreciation in the calculation of profit accord with the timing of the cash outflow on the initial investment. Although this method can be used to look at the effect on the return on capital to the company, it has been widely supplanted by one or other of the discounting methods of appraisal which now follow.

Net present value (NPV)

The NPV method discounts the yearly cash flows back to their present value either by use of a present value factor table (as in Appendix 1) or by using the facility built in as standard on spreadsheets. The discount rate used is the cost of capital or other hurdle rate used to allow for risk. A positive NPV means the investment is viable, a negative NPV that it is not viable. Applying this method to our cost saving example, using a 10 per cent real cost of capital, results in Figure 10.1, which shows a positive NPV of £1370. This positive NPV indicates a viable project.

Year	Capital cost	Running costs	Savings	Net cash flow	PV factors at 10%	Present value
	£	£	£	£		£
0	−10000			−10000	1.000	−10000
1		−5000	+8000	+3000	.909	+2727
2		−5000	+8000	+3000	.826	+2478
3		−5000	+8000	+3000	.751	+2253
4		−5000	+8000	+3000	.683	+2049
5		−5000	+8000	+3000	.621	+1863

(NPV) Net Present Value = +1370

Figure 10.1 *Calculation of the net present value in real terms at 10 per cent*

Where an appraisal is done in real terms, and the cash flows are constant each year from Year 1, it is possible to perform the calculations manually in a simpler way. Appendix 2 is another present value table which cumulates the present value factors year by year. If we read off Year 5 in the 10% column we find the cumulative factor 3.791, which is about the same as the total of the individual factors for Years 1–5 read from Appendix 1. Any slight difference is due to rounding. The appraisal can now be set out as:

Year	Net cash flows	PV factors at 10%	Present value
	£		£
0	−10000	1.000	−10,000
1–5	+3000	3.791	+11,373

Net Present Value (NPV)   +1373

Internal rate of return (IRR)

IRR is sometimes referred to as the discounted cash flow rate of return or DCF yield. This is the discount rate which equates the NPV to zero. You can find it manually by trial and error and interpolation, or you can find the IRR by using a spreadsheet which has this function built in. Using the trial and error approach on the above example, the next higher discount rate is chosen (11 per cent) and the NPV recalculated at this rate in Figure 10.2. Then an extrapolation is performed using the NPVs at both 10 per cent and 11 per cent to estimate where the IRR lies.

Year	Capital cost	Running costs	Savings	Net cash flow	PV factors at 11%	Present value
	£	£	£	£		£
0	−10000			−10000	1.000	−10000
1		−5000	+8000	+3000	.901	+2703
2		−5000	+8000	+3000	.812	+2436
3		−5000	+8000	+3000	.731	+2193
4		−5000	+8000	+3000	.659	+1977
5		−5000	+8000	+3000	.593	+1779

Net Present Value (NPV) = +1088

Figure 10.2 *Calculation of the net present value in real terms at 11 per cent*

The IRR can now be found by extrapolating the two NPVs at the different discount rates:

NPV at 11% discount rate   =   +£1088
NPV at 10% discount rate   =   +£1370
Therefore 1% difference   =   £282

To reduce the £1088 surplus to zero requires another 4 per cent (1088/282) in addition to the 11 per cent, making an IRR of 15 per cent. This can be proved by using a spreadsheet which would also provide decimal places on the interest rate. Beware of taking the answer too literally. Although decimal places are correct mathematically, we need to remember that the basic cash flows are only estimates and are usually subject to a degree of error.

As the cash flows are constant in this example, we could use the cumulative PV table in Appendix 2 to good effect to find the IRR. This is done by dividing the capital cost by the constant annual cash flow to give the cumulative factor:

$$Cumulative\ pv\ factor\ =\ \frac{capital\ cost}{constant\ cash\ flow}\ =\ \frac{£10,000}{£3000}\ =\ 3.333$$

This is now looked for on the five-year line of the table, where the nearest factor is 3.352 in the 15% column. This tells us that the IRR is 15 per cent.

We defined the IRR as the discount rate that results in a NPV of zero.

Another way of thinking about what the IRR represents is to describe it as the rate of return earned on the reducing capital balance year by year. This is illustrated in Figure 10.3 in a way that we might think a building society repayment mortgage works:

Year	Cash flow	15% interest	Capital repaid	Capital outstanding
	£	£	£	£
0	−10000			10000
1	+3000	1500	1500	8500
2	+3000	1275	1725	6775
3	+3000	1016	1984	4791
4	+3000	719	2281	2510
5	+3000	376	2624	(114)

Figure 10.3 *Calculating a 15 per cent (approx) real return on the reducing capital balance*

We see here that each year 15 per cent interest has been allowed on the capital outstanding at the previous year end. All the £10,000 capital has been repaid and a small surplus of £114 remains because the true rate of interest is fractionally higher than 15 per cent. This is a good way for you to think of what the IRR means but not an easy way to find it by trial and error! Using PV factors or a spreadsheet is much easier.

TAXATION

When appraising investments in the private sector, the effects of taxation must be taken into account. For limited companies, the tax in question is corporation tax, which has a standard rate of 33 per cent but tapers down to equate with the 25 per cent standard rate of income tax for companies with profits below £1.5m.

Profit for tax purposes is not quite the same as the profit shown in a company profit and loss account. Apart from a number of relatively minor items of expenditure which are not allowable against tax, the major difference is the treatment of depreciation.

When calculating the tax charge, the Inland Revenue requires a company to add back to profit any depreciation charged in the profit and loss account. The relevant capital allowances or writing down allowances are now deducted to determine the taxable profit.

These tax transactions must be incorporated into the yearly cash flows after allowing for a time lag on the payment of tax, typically one year in investment appraisals.

Taking the above example of the purchase of a machine for £10,000, this will be subject to capital allowances of 25 per cent each year based on the reducing balance method. Tax at 33 per cent is saved on these allowances. The net savings of £3000 in each year of the five-year life will also be subject to tax at the rate of 33 per cent. As no depreciation was allowed in the compilation of these net savings originally, we do not have to add any back in this case. This results in Figure 10.4, which shows the net cash flows after discounting, keeping the tax payments and savings separate for clarification.

The inclusion of taxation has reduced the size of the net cash flows compared with Figure 10.1 as the tax payments normally exceed the tax savings, as shown in this case. The new net cash flows are now discounted at the cost of capital (10 per cent real post-tax in our original example).

Year	Investment	Profit before depreciation	Tax paid at 33%	Capital allowance allowance	Tax saved on	Net cash flow	PV factors at 10%	Present value
	£	£	£	£	£	£		£
0	−10000					−10000	1.000	−10000
1		+3000		2500		+3000	.909	+2727
2		+3000	−990	1875	+825	+2835	.826	+2342
3		+3000	−990	1406	+619	+2629	.751	+1974
4		+3000	−990	1055	+464	+2474	.683	+1690
5		+3000	−990	3164*	+348	+2358	.621	+1464
6			−990		+1044	+54	.564	+30

Net Present Value (NPV) = +227

* The remaining capital allowances have been included in year 5 for this short-life asset.

Figure 10.4 *Incorporating taxation in the appraisal*

Inflation has a distorting effect on taxation and may affect costs and sales differently. Profits can be expected to increase in later years if not actually to keep in line with inflation. Corporation tax is levied on these inflated profits, but no increase in capital allowances is made each year to compensate for inflation.

A more precise way to set out cash flows is to inflate each element at the appropriate rate(s) and discount the nominal net cash flows at the nominal cost of capital. Conversely, the nominal net cash flows can be first deflated by a general price index and then discounted at the real cost of capital. Either of these approaches will deal adequately with the effects of inflation on tax and with any differential effects on costs and revenues.

UNCERTAINTY

One thing you can be certain of is that most estimated cash flows in appraisals will turn out to be incorrect. This was one reason for saying earlier that too much reliance should not be placed on decimal places in the IRR calculation. There are some relatively crude methods that can be used to reduce the risk inherent in an uncertain future, including:

- Setting a short payback criterion. This approach might reduce risk but it may also reject very profitable investments that are slow to get going, or are long lived.
- Preparing two further sets of cash flows based on pessimistic/optimistic parameters. This sets the outer limits within which the actual IRR should eventually occur.
- Varying the hurdle rate with an assessment of risk. This uses the trade-off between risk and reward, setting higher reward targets for higher-risk projects. This can be based on the CAPM approach mentioned earlier in the context of cost of capital.
- Using conservative values of future cash flows.

Drury et al[2] found that the most widely used techniques for dealing with risk were sensitivity analysis (see below), adjusting the payback period and using conservative estimates of cash flows.

More scientific methods can be used on important project appraisals where the capital to be invested is significant in relation to the size of the organization. Computers have an important role to play here when repetitive calculations are involved in simulations and probability analysis. Drury found little evidence of their regular use, nor for the use of betas (CAPM) as a risk measure on a project.

Sensitivity analysis

One very practical way to assess the effects of uncertainty is to use *sensitivity analysis*. This approach tests the effect on the NPV or IRR for a chosen degree of error of any one variable in the cash flow model. This is repeated in turn for each variable so that the key variables can be identified. Once they are known, estimates can be refined and more data collected before firming up on a final estimate for each variable. If the project gets the go-ahead and is implemented, these key variables are the ones that need monitoring from time to time to ensure the project's continued success.

The variables in any cost-saving investment will include:

■ capital cost;
■ operating costs;
■ savings;
■ life of equipment;
■ residual value of equipment (if any);
■ rate of taxation;
■ rate of capital allowances;
■ rate(s) of inflation on variables.

Selecting life, operating costs and savings as key variables in our earlier cost saving investment, the matrix in Figure 10.5 now shows the IRRs for each of these variables within parameters that vary 20 per cent either way.

	Life	Running costs	Savings
Original values	5 years	£5000	£8000
IRR on expected value of all variables	15%	15%	15%
IRR when one variable is 20% better	20%	29%	36%
IRR when one variable is 20% worse	8%	0%	(–)ve

Figure 10.5 *Sensitivity of IRR to variations in independent key variables*

Sensitivity tests in this example show that inaccuracies in the estimates of the savings variable affect the return on the investment more than inaccuracies in the running costs variable, which itself is more sensitive than the life of the project. The worse case for any one of these variables results in an IRR less than the real cost of capital of 10 per cent.

A further sensitivity test could be carried out to determine the minimum value, for each variable independently, that is needed to give the required minimum return of 10 per cent. In each case the other two variables are held at their original estimates.

Drury et al[2] found that 82 per cent of the larger manufacturing organizations sampled, often or always used sensitivity analysis when allowing for risk.

POST-COMPLETION AUDIT (PCA)

It is important for the capital expenditure on projects to be monitored on a regular basis during the development phase. Top management should be advised of both spend-to-date and forecast-to-completion for every large individual project and by each category for smaller projects. This allows projects to be aborted or modified, if necessary, when they are not proceeding according to the amount budgeted. This monitoring process is explicit in organizations with formalized capital budgeting procedures.

Additionally, *post-completion auditing* requires actual costs and benefits, and the premises on which they were based, to be compared with their original estimates once a project is fully implemented. This process can be carried out formally or informally.

The informal approach applies where each project sponsor re-examines the project for feedback on whether the project is working to plan or not, thus highlighting the need for future modifications. Such feedback will also give information for the preparation of similar schemes in the future.

The formal approach uses the term 'audit' in its normal sense. CIMA defines a post-completion audit as 'an objective and independent approval of the measure of success of a capital expenditure project in progressing the business as planned. The appraisal should cover the implementation of the project from authorization to commissioning and its technical and commercial performance after commissioning.'

Would you agree that the existence of such a system will influence you and other managers to take a more realistic and rigourous attitude to the preparation of estimates and the appraisal techniques employed? Neale[3] found that 79 per cent of a large sample drawn from the *Times 1000* listing used post-audits. This represented a jump from under 50 per cent five years previously.

SUMMARY

This chapter introduced the idea that the cost of the capital sets the minimum return needed on any proposed investment for it to be financially worthwhile. This cost of capital is incorporated in investment appraisals as the discount rate used in NPV calculations or in assessing if the IRR is satisfactory. These methods of appraisal are superior to the accounting rate of return and payback, although the latter is still widely used in capital rationing or risk reduction settings.

You may find in your own organization that a combination of appraisal methods is used. A survey by Pike and Wolfe of 100 large UK industrial companies showed that over one-third of firms claimed to use all four appraisal techniques.[4]

Profit-seeking organizations need to take tax into account when examining the profitability of new investments. The timing of tax allowances will help to soften the impact of tax payments on long-life projects. Broadly speaking, the incorporation of tax will normally have a negative effect on the IRR.

All organizations should take account of uncertainty in their appraisal systems. One can never forecast the future with certainty and allowance should be made for what could go wrong and how damaging that might be to the viability of the project. It is better to consider all the pros and cons before investing, because once the capital is spent there is often no going back and few investments are recovered in full if they have to be aborted.

One final point: the survey by Drury et al[2] found that only 27 per cent of the manufacturing organizations sampled dealt with inflation correctly. This emphasizes the need to match real or nominal cash flows to real or nominal discount rates respectively.

References

1. Pike, R H and Ho, S (1991) 'Risk analysis in capital budgeting contexts: simple or sophisticated', *Accounting and Business Research*, Summer.

2. Drury, C, Braund, S, Osborne, P, and Tayles, M (1993) *A survey of management accounting practices in UK manufacturing companies*, ACCA, London.

3. Neale, C W (1991) 'A revolution in post-completion audit adoption', *Management Accounting* (UK), November.

4. Pike, R H and Wolfe, M B (1988) *Capital budgeting for the 1990's*, CIMA, London.

Appendix 1 Present value of £1

n Year	5%	6%	7%	8%	9%	10%	11%	12%	13%	14%	15%	16%	17%	18%	19%	20%	21%	22%	23%	24%	25%	26%	27%	28%	29%	30%	35%	40%
0	1.000	1.000	1.000	1.000	1.000	1.000	1.000	1.000	1.000	1.000	1.000	1.000	1.000	1.000	1.000	1.000	1.000	1.000	1.000	1.000	1.000	1.000	1.000	1.000	1.000	1.000	1.000	1.000
1	.952	.943	.935	.926	.917	.909	.901	.893	.885	.877	.870	.862	.855	.846	.840	.833	.826	.820	.813	.807	.800	.794	.787	.781	.775	.769	.741	.714
2	.907	.890	.873	.857	.842	.826	.812	.797	.783	.769	.756	.743	.731	.718	.706	.694	.683	.672	.661	.650	.640	.630	.620	.610	.601	.592	.549	.510
3	.864	.840	.816	.794	.772	.751	.731	.712	.693	.675	.658	.641	.624	.609	.593	.579	.564	.551	.537	.524	.512	.500	.488	.477	.466	.455	.406	.364
4	.823	.792	.763	.735	.708	.683	.659	.636	.613	.592	.572	.552	.534	.516	.499	.482	.467	.451	.437	.423	.410	.397	.384	.373	.361	.350	.301	.260
5	.784	.747	.713	.681	.650	.621	.593	.567	.543	.519	.497	.476	.456	.437	.419	.402	.386	.370	.355	.341	.328	.315	.303	.291	.280	.269	.223	.186
6	.746	.705	.666	.630	.596	.564	.535	.507	.480	.456	.432	.410	.390	.370	.352	.335	.319	.303	.289	.275	.262	.250	.238	.227	.217	.207	.165	.133
7	.711	.665	.623	.583	.547	.513	.482	.452	.425	.400	.376	.354	.333	.314	.296	.279	.263	.249	.235	.222	.210	.198	.188	.178	.168	.159	.122	.095
8	.677	.627	.582	.540	.502	.467	.434	.404	.376	.351	.327	.305	.285	.266	.249	.233	.218	.204	.191	.179	.168	.157	.148	.139	.130	.123	.091	.068
9	.645	.592	.544	.500	.460	.424	.391	.361	.333	.308	.284	.263	.243	.225	.209	.194	.180	.167	.155	.144	.134	.125	.116	.108	.101	.094	.067	.048
10	.614	.558	.508	.463	.422	.386	.352	.322	.295	.270	.247	.227	.208	.191	.176	.162	.149	.137	.126	.116	.107	.099	.092	.085	.078	.073	.050	.035
11	.585	.527	.475	.429	.388	.350	.317	.287	.261	.237	.215	.195	.178	.162	.148	.135	.123	.112	.103	.094	.086	.079	.072	.066	.061	.056	.037	.025
12	.557	.497	.444	.397	.356	.319	.286	.257	.231	.208	.187	.168	.152	.137	.124	.112	.102	.092	.083	.076	.069	.062	.057	.052	.047	.043	.027	.018
13	.530	.469	.415	.368	.326	.290	.258	.229	.204	.182	.163	.145	.130	.116	.104	.093	.084	.075	.068	.061	.055	.050	.045	.040	.037	.033	.020	.013
14	.505	.442	.388	.340	.299	.263	.232	.205	.181	.160	.141	.125	.111	.099	.088	.078	.069	.062	.055	.049	.044	.039	.035	.032	.028	.025	.015	.009
15	.481	.417	.362	.315	.275	.239	.209	.183	.160	.140	.123	.108	.095	.084	.074	.065	.057	.051	.045	.040	.035	.031	.028	.025	.022	.020	.011	.006
16	.458	.394	.339	.292	.252	.218	.188	.163	.141	.123	.107	.093	.081	.071	.062	.054	.047	.042	.036	.032	.028	.025	.022	.019	.017	.015	.008	.005
17	.436	.371	.317	.270	.231	.198	.170	.146	.125	.108	.093	.080	.069	.060	.052	.045	.039	.034	.030	.026	.023	.020	.017	.015	.013	.012	.006	.003
18	.416	.350	.296	.250	.212	.180	.153	.130	.111	.095	.081	.069	.059	.051	.044	.038	.032	.028	.024	.021	.018	.016	.014	.012	.010	.009	.005	.002
19	.396	.331	.277	.232	.194	.164	.138	.116	.098	.083	.070	.060	.051	.043	.037	.031	.027	.023	.020	.017	.014	.012	.011	.009	.008	.007	.003	.002
20	.377	.312	.258	.215	.178	.149	.124	.104	.087	.073	.061	.051	.043	.037	.031	.026	.022	.019	.016	.014	.012	.010	.008	.007	.006	.005	.002	.001
25	.295	.233	.184	.146	.116	.092	.074	.059	.047	.038	.030	.025	.020	.016	.013	.011	.009	.007	.006	.005	.004	.003	.003	.002	.002	.001	.001	.000
30	.231	.174	.131	.099	.075	.057	.044	.033	.026	.020	.015	.012	.009	.007	.005	.004	.003	.003	.002	.002	.001	.001	.001	.000	.000	.000	.000	.000
35	.181	.130	.094	.068	.049	.036	.026	.019	.014	.010	.008	.006	.004	.003	.002	.002	.001	.001	.001	.001	.000	.000	.000	.000	.000	.000	.000	.000
40	.142	.097	.067	.046	.032	.022	.015	.011	.008	.005	.004	.003	.002	.001	.001	.001	.001	.000	.000	.000	.000	.000	.000	.000	.000	.000	.000	.000
45	.111	.073	.048	.031	.021	.014	.009	.006	.004	.003	.002	.001	.001	.001	.001	.000	.000	.000	.000	.000	.000	.000	.000	.000	.000	.000	.000	.000
50	.087	.054	.034	.021	.013	.009	.005	.003	.002	.001	.001	.001	.000	.000	.000	.000	.000	.000	.000	.000	.000	.000	.000	.000	.000	.000	.000	.000

Note   The above present value factors are based on year-end interest calculations.

Appendix 2 Cumulative present value of £1 per annum

n Year	5%	6%	7%	8%	9%	10%	11%	12%	13%	14%	15%	16%	17%	18%	19%	20%	21%	22%	23%	24%	25%	26%	27%	28%	29%	30%	35%	40%
1	.952	.943	.935	.926	.917	.909	.901	.893	.885	.877	.870	.862	.855	.847	.840	.833	.826	.820	.813	.807	.800	.794	.787	.781	.775	.769	.741	.714
2	1.859	1.833	1.808	1.783	1.759	1.736	1.713	1.690	1.668	1.647	1.626	1.605	1.585	1.566	1.546	1.528	1.510	1.492	1.474	1.457	1.440	1.424	1.407	1.392	1.376	1.361	1.289	1.224
3	2.723	2.673	2.624	2.577	2.531	2.487	2.444	2.402	2.361	2.322	2.283	2.246	2.210	2.174	2.140	2.106	2.074	2.042	2.011	1.981	1.952	1.923	1.896	1.868	1.842	1.816	1.696	1.589
4	3.546	3.465	3.387	3.312	3.240	3.170	3.102	3.037	2.974	2.914	2.855	2.798	2.743	2.690	2.639	2.589	2.540	2.494	2.448	2.404	2.362	2.320	2.280	2.241	2.203	2.166	1.997	1.849
5	4.329	4.212	4.100	3.993	3.890	3.791	3.696	3.605	3.517	3.433	3.352	3.274	3.199	3.127	3.058	2.991	2.926	2.864	2.804	2.745	2.689	2.635	2.583	2.532	2.483	2.436	2.220	2.035
6	5.076	4.917	4.767	4.623	4.486	4.355	4.231	4.111	3.998	3.889	3.784	3.685	3.589	3.498	3.410	3.326	3.245	3.167	3.092	3.021	2.951	2.885	2.821	2.759	2.700	2.643	2.385	2.168
7	5.786	5.582	5.389	5.206	5.033	4.868	4.712	4.564	4.423	4.288	4.160	4.039	3.922	3.812	3.706	3.605	3.508	3.416	3.327	3.242	3.161	3.083	3.009	2.937	2.868	2.802	2.508	2.263
8	6.463	6.210	5.971	5.747	5.535	5.335	5.146	4.968	4.799	4.639	4.487	4.344	4.207	4.078	3.954	3.837	3.726	3.619	3.518	3.421	3.329	3.241	3.156	3.076	2.999	2.925	2.598	2.331
9	7.108	6.802	6.515	6.247	5.995	5.759	5.537	5.328	5.132	4.946	4.772	4.607	4.451	4.303	4.163	4.031	3.905	3.786	3.673	3.566	3.463	3.366	3.273	3.184	3.100	3.019	2.665	2.379
10	7.722	7.360	7.024	6.710	6.418	6.145	5.889	5.650	5.426	5.216	5.019	4.833	4.659	4.494	4.339	4.192	4.054	3.923	3.799	3.682	3.571	3.465	3.366	3.269	3.178	3.092	2.715	2.414
11	8.306	7.887	7.499	7.139	6.805	6.495	6.207	5.938	5.687	5.453	5.234	5.029	4.836	4.656	4.486	4.327	4.177	4.035	3.902	3.776	3.656	3.544	3.437	3.335	3.239	3.147	2.752	2.438
12	8.863	8.384	7.943	7.536	7.161	6.814	6.492	6.194	5.918	5.660	5.421	5.197	4.988	4.793	4.610	4.439	4.278	4.127	3.985	3.851	3.725	3.606	3.493	3.387	3.286	3.190	2.779	2.456
13	9.394	8.853	8.358	7.904	7.487	7.103	6.750	6.424	6.122	5.842	5.583	5.342	5.118	4.910	4.715	4.533	4.362	4.203	4.053	3.912	3.780	3.656	3.538	3.427	3.322	3.223	2.799	2.469
14	9.899	9.295	8.745	8.244	7.786	7.367	6.982	6.628	6.302	6.002	5.724	5.468	5.229	5.008	4.802	4.611	4.432	4.265	4.108	3.962	3.824	3.695	3.573	3.459	3.351	3.249	2.814	2.478
15	10.380	9.712	9.108	8.559	8.061	7.606	7.191	6.811	6.462	6.142	5.847	5.575	5.324	5.092	4.876	4.675	4.490	4.315	4.153	4.001	3.859	3.726	3.601	3.483	3.373	3.268	2.825	2.484
16	10.838	10.106	9.447	8.851	8.313	7.824	7.379	6.974	6.604	6.265	5.954	5.669	5.405	5.162	4.938	4.730	4.536	4.357	4.190	4.033	3.887	3.751	3.623	3.503	3.390	3.283	2.834	2.489
17	11.274	10.477	9.763	9.122	8.544	8.022	7.549	7.120	6.729	6.373	6.047	5.749	5.475	5.222	4.990	4.775	4.576	4.391	4.219	4.059	3.910	3.771	3.640	3.518	3.403	3.295	2.840	2.492
18	11.690	10.828	10.059	9.372	8.756	8.201	7.702	7.250	6.840	6.467	6.128	5.818	5.534	5.273	5.033	4.812	4.608	4.419	4.243	4.080	3.928	3.786	3.654	3.529	3.413	3.304	2.844	2.494
19	12.085	11.158	10.366	9.604	8.950	8.365	7.839	7.366	6.938	6.550	6.198	5.877	5.584	5.316	5.070	4.844	4.635	4.442	4.263	4.097	3.942	3.799	3.666	3.539	3.421	3.311	2.848	2.496
20	12.462	11.470	10.594	9.818	9.129	8.514	7.963	7.469	7.025	6.623	6.259	5.929	5.628	5.353	5.101	4.870	4.657	4.460	4.279	4.110	3.954	3.808	3.673	3.546	3.427	3.316	2.850	2.497
25	14.094	12.783	11.654	10.675	9.823	9.077	8.422	7.843	7.330	6.873	6.464	6.097	5.766	5.467	5.195	4.948	4.721	4.514	4.323	4.147	3.985	3.834	3.694	3.564	3.442	3.329	2.856	2.499
30	15.372	13.765	12.409	11.258	10.274	9.427	8.694	8.055	7.496	7.003	6.566	6.177	5.829	5.517	5.235	4.979	4.746	4.534	4.339	4.160	3.995	3.842	3.701	3.569	3.447	3.332	2.857	2.500
35	16.374	14.498	12.948	11.655	10.567	9.644	8.855	8.176	7.586	7.070	6.617	6.215	5.858	5.539	5.251	4.992	4.756	4.541	4.345	4.164	3.998	3.845	3.703	3.571	3.448	3.333	2.857	2.500
40	17.159	15.046	13.332	11.925	10.757	9.779	8.951	8.244	7.634	7.105	6.642	6.234	5.871	5.548	5.258	4.997	4.760	4.544	4.347	4.166	3.999	3.846	3.703	3.571	3.448	3.333	2.857	2.500
45	17.774	15.456	13.606	12.108	10.881	9.863	9.008	8.283	7.661	7.123	6.654	6.242	5.877	5.552	5.261	4.999	4.761	4.545	4.347	4.166	4.000	3.846	3.704	3.571	3.448	3.333	2.857	2.500
50	18.256	15.762	13.801	12.234	10.962	9.915	9.042	8.305	7.675	7.133	6.661	6.246	5.880	5.554	5.262	5.000	4.762	4.545	4.348	4.167	4.000	3.846	3.704	3.571	3.448	3.333	2.857	2.500

Note The above present value factors are based on year-end interest calculations.

Bibliography

Barrow, C, Barrow, P and Brown, R (1992) *The Business Plan Workbook*, Kogan Page, London.

Blake, J (1993) *Accounting Standards*, Pitman, London.

Blake, J and Amat, O (1993) *European Accounting*, Pitman, London.

Drury, C (1993) *Management and Cost Accounting*, Chapman & Hall, London.

Fitzgerald, L, Johnston, R, Brignall, S, Silvestro, R and Voss, C (1991) *Performance Measurement in Service Businesses*, CIMA, London.

Garbutt, D (1992) *Making Budgets Work*, CIMA, London.

Hammer, M and Champy, J (1993) *Re-engineering the Corporation*, Nicholas Brealey, London.

Johansson, H T (1993) *Business Process Re-engineering*, Wiley, Chichester.

Johnson, H T and Kaplan, R S (1987) *Relevance Lost: The Rise and Fall of Management Accounting*, Harvard Business School Press.

Jones, R and Pendlebury, M (1992) *Public Sector Accounting*, Pitman, London.

Lewis, R W and Pendmill, D (1991) *Advanced Financial Accounting*, Pitman, London.

Mott, G (1991) *Management Accounting for Decision Makers*, Pitman, London.

Mott, G (1993) *Investment Appraisal*, Pitman, London.

Murphy, J (1991) *Brand Valuation*, Business Books.

Neale, B and Holmes, D (1991) *Post-completion Auditing*, Pitman, London.

Pike, R H and Dobbins, R (1986) *Investment Decisions and Financial Strategy*, Philip Allan, Oxford.

Smith, T (1992) *Accounting for Growth*, Century Business, London.

Westwick, C A (1987) *How to Use Management Ratios*, Gower, Aldershot.

Performance Measurement in the Manufacturing Sector (1993) Combined study by CIMA, NIMTEC and Cambridge, Warwick and Glasgow Universities.

Glossary

Absorption costing   A system of costing where cost units (products) absorb a share of indirect costs in addition to their direct costs.

Accrual Outstanding expenses for an accounting period for which the invoice has not been received and therefore not paid.

Acid test ratio   A measure of liquidity obtained by dividing debtors, cash and short-term investments by current liabilities (short-term creditors).

Activity-based costing (ABC)   The identification of activities as a basis for charging overhead costs to cost units (products).

Advance corporation tax   A part of the total corporation tax liability which is paid to the Inland Revenue at the time a dividend is paid to shareholders.

Asset   Any possession or claim on others which is of value to a firm. *See also* fixed assets and current assets.

Associated company   A company in which another company owns a substantial shareholding exceeding 20 per cent but not more than 50 per cent of the total.

Balance sheet   A statement of the financial position of a firm at a particular date showing the assets owned and the sources of finance.

Benchmarking   A comparison with best practice in order to help to gain superior performance.

Book value   The original or historical cost of an asset less accumulated depreciation.

Break-even point   The level of output or sales value at which total costs equal total revenues.

Budgetary control   Financial plans to meet objectives in the accounting year against which actual results are compared.

Capital allowance   The Inland Revenue's equivalent of a company's depreciation charge. Allowances are granted on purchases of certain new assets and reduce the taxable profits.

Capital employed   The permanent and long-term capital used by a firm comprising share capital, reserves, and long-term loans in the case of a limited company. This is also equal to total assets less current liabilities.

Capital reserves   *See* reserves.

Cash flow   The definition depends on the context in which the term is used but is generally regarded as the operating profit after adding back the depreciation charge for the period.

Cash flow statement   A financial statement showing the internal and external sources and uses of cash during a period.

Consolidated accounts   A combined profit and loss account and a combined balance sheet for a holding company and its subsidiaries.

Contribution   The difference between sales and the variable cost of the goods sold, before charging fixed costs.

Convertible loan   Starts its life as a conventional loan but gives the holder the right to transfer into a specified number of ordinary shares at a later date.

Corporation tax   Tax levied on a limited company's profit. There is one standard rate (currently 33 per cent), but a small company rate applies to those companies with insufficient profit to be taxed at the higher level.

Cost centre   A physical location within an organization, for example a department or section, where costs are accumulated.

Cost code   A numbering system used to describe the type, source, and purpose of all costs and revenues.

Cost—direct or indirect   A direct cost is one which can be specifically allocated to a product, as in the case of materials used and labour expended. An indirect cost cannot be directly related to any particular product but is more general in nature. Indirect costs are alternatively called overheads and direct costs are sometimes referred to as prime costs.

Cost unit   Any product or service to which costs can be charged.

Cost—variable or fixed   A variable cost varies in total to the volume of production. A fixed cost stays the same total sum over a range of output levels.

Creditor   Any party to whom the business owes money, separated into amounts payable within and after one year, and usually analyzed into borrowings and other creditors.

Current assets   Cash and other short-term assets in the process of being turned back into cash, for example stocks and debtors.

Current cost accounting   A procedure for adjusting items in a company profit and loss account and balance sheet for the effects of inflation.

Current liabilities   Creditors payable within one year, for example trade creditors, bank overdrafts, dividends, and tax provisions.

Current ratio   A measure of liquidity obtained by dividing current assets by current liabilities.

Debtor   A credit customer (trade debtor) or other party who owes money to the firm.

Debt ratio   The relationship of total debts to total assets.

Deferred tax   Tax which is not payable at one specific time but which may become payable at a future date.

Depreciation   A proportion of the cost of a fixed asset charged as an expense in a company profit and loss account.

Differential costing   The costs and/or revenues of alternative courses of action which are compared to identify the differences between them.

Discounted cash flow (DCF)   A method used to calculate the present value of cash flows, taking into account the time value of money.

Dividend   A periodic distribution to shareholders in proportion to the number of shares held.

Dividend cover   A measure of the security of the dividend payment obtained by dividing the profit after tax by the total dividend.

Dividend yield   The income obtained from the gross dividend as a percentage of the current market price of a share.

Double entry bookkeeping   The method of recording financial transactions whereby every item is entered as a debit in one account and a corresponding credit in another.

Earnings per share   Profit after tax earned for shareholders divided by the number of ordinary shares issued.

Earnings yield   The earnings per share expressed as a percentage of the current market price of an ordinary share.

Equity   *See* shareholders' funds.

Factoring   The receipt of cash from a specialist company against the security of sales invoices which that company collects.

Fixed assets   Assets used by the firm itself and not sold in the normal course of business. For example, buildings and plants and machinery.

Flexible budget   A budget which is constructed to change in accordance with the actual level of activity achieved.

Gearing   The relationship of borrowings to shareholders' funds.

Goodwill   The benefit accruing to a business because of its name and reputation. When another business is acquired, goodwill is the difference between the the purchase price and the value of the net assets acquired.

Gross profit   The difference between sales and the cost of goods sold before charging general overhead expenses.

Gross profit margin   Gross profit expressed as a percentage of sales.

Group accounts   *See* consolidated accounts.

Historical cost accounting   The recording of transactions at the actual cost incurred at the time of purchase, irrespective of the item's current value.

Holding company   The parent company which owns a controlling interest in one or more subsidiaries.

Inflation accounting   *See* current cost accounting.

Intangible assets   Assets of a non-physical nature including goodwill, patents, trade marks, brands and royalty agreements.

Internal rate of return (IRR)   A measure of the true rate of profitability expected on a project. It represents the maximum rate of interest which could be paid on the diminishing capital balance of an investment.

Investment centre   A type of responsibility centre where the manager is responsible for revenues, costs, profit and investment, culminating in either a residual profit or return on capital objective.

Mainstream corporation tax   The balance of the tax liability after the advance payments have been made.

Marginal costing   A system of costing used for decision making which is based on the analysis of costs into fixed and variable categories.

Market capitalization   The total market value of all a quoted company's ordinary shares.

Minority interests   The proportion of a subsidiary company which is owned by outside shareholders as opposed to the parent or holding company. Cannot apply to wholly owned subsidiaries.

Net present value (NPV)   The sum of all the negative and positive present values of the cash flows in an investment appraisal, indicating that project's viability when they are positive.

Net profit before taxation   The profit after all costs (including interest) have been deducted, but before tax and dividends.

Net profit after taxation   The profit after all costs, interests and taxation have been deducted but before dividends.

Net profit margin   Net profit before interest, tax and dividends expressed as a percentage of sales.

Ordinary shares   The class of capital entitling the holders to all remaining profits after all costs, interest and preference dividends have been paid. They are also entitled to all residual assets once other claimants have been repaid on liquidation.

Outsourcing   The buying-in of services, components or manufactured goods.

Overtrading   A liquidity problem caused by insufficient working capital to support the level of sales.

Payback period   The number of years taken to recover the original sum invested.

Post-completion audit   A comparison of the original estimates and premises on which they were based with the actual outcomes of an investment project.

Preference shares   The class of capital entitling the holders to a fixed rate of dividend prior to any ordinary share dividend. On liquidation holders are also entitled to the repayment of their capital before ordinary shareholders are repaid.

Present value   The equivalent value now of a sum of money receivable in a later year.

Price/earnings ratio A ratio used for comparing market prices of different companies' ordinary shares. It is calculated by dividing the market price of the share by the earnings per share.

Profit and loss account (or income statement) It summarizes the revenue and expenditure of a company to arrive at the net profit or loss for the period.

Profit centre A type of responsibility centre where the manager is responsible for costs and revenues and therefore profit, but without authority for the level of investment.

Profit margin A ratio used to measure performance, calculated by expressing gross or net profit as a percentage of sales value.

Ratio Two figures usually extracted from the profit and loss account and/or balance sheet and related together as a percentage, ratio or function.

Realization An accounting concept which states that profit is earned when a sale takes place and not when cash from that sale is received. It is also referred to as the accruals concept.

Reserves Revenue reserves are retained profits. Capital reserves occur when fixed assets are revalued or sold at a profit and when a company sells new shares at a premium. Revenue reserves (but not capital reserves) may be distributed in the form of dividends.

Return on capital (ROC) Profit before tax and interest charges expressed as a percentage of capital employed.

Revenue centre A type of responsibility centre where the manager is responsible for the revenue generated from sales.

Rights issue An invitation to existing shareholders to subscribe for new shares when a company requires further capital.

Scrip issue A free or bonus issue of new shares to existing shareholders in proportion to their existing holding. No new capital is received by the company which translates existing reserves into share capital.

Sensitivity analysis Used in investment appraisal as a risk technique where any component in the net cash flows can be examined for its effect on the NPV or the IRR when its value is varied from the original estimate.

Share capital Money subscribed by shareholders in a limited company for ordinary or preference shares. Issued share capital is the amount of capital actually received, while authorized capital is the total amount the directors are empowered to issue.

Share premium account   The extra cash received by a company when it sells shares for more than their par value. It is a capital reserve and must be distinguished from the issued share capital in the balance sheet.

Shareholders' funds or net worth   The total amount of shareholders' investment in the company, comprising issued share capital, retained profits, and all other reserves. It equals the value of all the company's assets after deducting all debts owing to outside parties. Other terms with the same meaning include 'share capital and reserves', 'shareholders' equity' or 'net assets'.

Standard costing   A system of costing whereby predetermined product costs are compared with actual costs to highlight significant variances which are then investigated.

Subsidiary   A company which is controlled by another company which owns more than 50 per cent of the voting shares.

Trial balance   The list of debit and credit balances on individual accounts from which a profit and loss account and balance sheet are prepared.

Turnover   An alternative word for sales or revenue.

Turnover of capital   The relationship of sales to capital employed, stating the number of times each £1 of capital has generated £1 of sales in one year.

Value added statement   A financial statement showing the wealth created by a company in a period of time and how it was distributed to the interested parties.

Variance   The difference between a budget or standard and the actual amount.

Virement   Where a manager is allowed to switch budgeted amounts from one cost heading to another.

Working capital   That part of a firm's total capital which is tied up in stocks, work in progress and debtors less short-term obligations such as creditors and bank overdrafts. It is equal to current assets less current liabilities.

Z score   A combination of certain accounting ratios used to predict business failure.

Zero based budget   A budget compiled without reference to the prior year's budget.

Index